the
tyranny
of the group

the tyranny of the group

by Andrew Malcolm M.D.

Clarke, Irwin & Company Limited / Toronto / Vancouver

© 1973 by Andrew I. Malcolm

ISBN 0-7720-0622-9

1 2 3 4 5   JD   77 76 75 74 73

Printed in Canada

To Barbara

CONTENTS

Carl Rogers has observed that "the intensive group experience is perhaps the most significant social invention cf this century." Such claims are intriguing because they are so extravagant. They are put in such a way as to excite extreme reactions. They are designed to separate the benighted sceptics from the true believers.

I have long been fascinated by people's tendency to believe, exaggerate, and press on everyone else their new systems of truth. In the late 'forties, when I was an undergraduate medical student, a few members of a protestant sect attempted to recruit me into what they called their "fellowship". Several of my friends were similarly approached and a couple of them were persuaded to follow the teachings of the sect. A great deal of kindness was brought to bear on me but I continued to protest. The ultimate argument of the believers was what was interesting. They said that if I had never experienced the joy of salvation I was not in a position to reject the revealed word of God. I am sure that most people are threatened by this same argument more than once during their adolescence and the example is not, in itself, of great significance.

A few years later I became a resident in psychiatry at the New York Hospital, where nearly all my fellow residents were bogged down in their personal analytic quagmires. These excellent and learned fellows were outraged by my resistance to the Freudian vision of psychosexual truth. I would say nasty things about the primal horde, and penis envy, and the Oedipus business, and they would defend themselves just as though they had a strong position. It was their ultimate defence that really intrigued me. They said I was in no position to reject the principles of analytic determinism because I had not myself been subjected to the agonies and joys of the couch.

In the early 'sixties I joined the staff of the Addiction Research Foundation in Toronto and began to treat users of a variety of psychoactive drugs. In the course of the next few years I accumulated a good deal of clinical experience and read much of the literature in this highly specialized field. The ultimate charge of the acid-head gave me a very warm and comfortable feeling. I could not possibly know anything about acid unless I had myself swallowed this ambrosial drug on numerous occasions. Similarly I could know nothing at all about heroin unless I was myself a junkie; about the amphetamines unless I was myself a speed freak; or about the barbiturates unless I myself was hopelessly dependent on goofballs.

It was at about this time that I began to take a particular interest in cults and the characteristics of the true believer. Most importantly, I recognized that the proponents and proselytizers of greatest vigour were those who had come to subscribe most uncritically to the values of the cult and that, conversely, the most rational and convincing critics of the cult were people who had somehow managed not to be saved.

It was in the late 'sixties that the executives of the Addiction Research Foundation began to show an interest in that branch of the Human Potential Movement known as Organization Development. In the course of time the A.R.F.'s involvement in this field greatly intensified. A human-potential or growth centre was chosen, in this case the Quetico Centre on the north shore of Lake Superior, and over the next four years staff members were despatched to that wilderness retreat in the interest of organizational excellence.

As I had had some experience with enthusiasts in the past, my reaction to this programme tended to be sceptical. I did some reading and prepared a series of papers on the T-group and its many successors. In these papers I drew attention particularly to certain aspects of the Human Potential Movement that I felt were undesirable, or required at the very least research and careful consideration. Among the believers this series of papers was not popular, but it was their ultimate charge that I found most interesting. They said that I was being irrationally resistive and should not presume to criticize the programme unless I had myself been processed by the trainers at the Quetico Centre.

Belief systems are like that. They are based on ideas that are held to be self-evidently true. And as they are self-evident there is obviously no need to prove that they are true. "To those who do not believe no explanation is possible." Unless, of course, through the application of a variety of techniques of persuasion the resistant, pitiable and unnerving unbeliever can be caused to confess the errors of his ways and proceed unswervingly in the direction of the light.

It is certainly not easy to oppose the fashions of whatever culture one happens to be living in at any point in time. It is far more comfortable to become a Christian, an orthodox Freudian analyst, a user of the illusionogens, or a devotee of group think, whenever such adherence seems expedient. Of course, I should also say that if the pressures brought to bear on the deviant person are not unduly severe, his scepticism may make his life more interesting. This has always been my case and therefore I lay no claim to any undue amount of fortitude. For many people, however, the stakes have been, and still are, vastly higher.

Living in Nazi Germany during the 'thirties, you would have had to be a very courageous person not to conform at least outwardly to the beliefs and behaviour promoted by the regime. In fact you would probably not have survived. In Germany your deviation from official group norms would have been identified as a species of criminality, and you would have been dealt with accordingly. In our decidedly safer society about all you have to endure is the possibility of dismissal from your work, a certain amount of social ostracism, and some rather funny name calling. Still, for many people, these threats are very serious indeed. They are confusing and disruptive, and the threatened person soon realizes that conformity is far safer than deviance.

If a sheep is conditioned to expect food when he perceives a perfectly circular image he is contented and at ease. He also learns that when a square image is presented he must not approach the food or else he will suffer some unpleasantness, for example an electric shock. If, however, after the experimenter has firmly established these positive and negative stimuli in the sheep's mind, he begins to round the corners of the square and flatten the circle, the sheep will become progressively more hesitant, uncertain and uncomfortable. Finally the square will be so rounded as to be almost indistinguishable from the angled circle. The sheep will be paralyzed with anxiety and quite unable to know what to do. He will show all sorts of neurotic behaviour because his secure understanding of what is good and what is bad has been utterly shattered. The sheep would be far more comfortable if he could only be shown a nice safe circle. He could then advance confidently to the food knowing that he would not be punished.

So it is with people. They try to know where they stand so that they will gain approval rather than condemnation. For most people an important source of approval comes from the group with which they are associated and whose peculiar language they understand. They belong there. And everyone who has not yet been initiated into this preferred cult is described by such progressively threatening terms as "square", "deviant", "criminal", "subhuman".

The encounterist, for example, considers himself to be at the very growing edge of the cultural revolution, and so he would suggest unkindly that all people not at the very growing edge are joylessly square. And in need of processing. He would feel this way particularly about any outsider who presumed to question the usefulness of his encounter culture's vision of the ideal society. He would suggest that such a critic is disqualified by his status as an outsider.

I am such an outsider and it will therefore be necessary for me to show that such a person may be better qualified to criticize any social movement than would be either an active participant or a disillusioned defector. The best answer, I would say, is that all three have something useful to say. The believer, in the midst of the mill, would tend to be passionate in his presentation of the beauty and utility of the thing. The defector, disillusioned and hostile, would be suspected of axe-grinding and narrowness of purpose. He would have the advantage, nevertheless, of having been through the mill, and many people would find his credibility better for the experience.

I am not now in the mill nor have I ever had the slightest desire to be ground in it. I have conducted group psychotherapy sessions for many years and observed the complex processes of group interaction; but this, I can assure my readers, is an experience that the encounterist would discount as a thing of no value whatsoever. Psychiatric group psychotherapy, he would say, is to the gut-level encounter what a tranquilizer is to LSD. I have observed the Synanon Game in savage action in Santa Monica and I have watched the encounter in process in a variety of places over quite a number of years. Nothing. I have not crawled on the floor, weeping and gnashing my teeth; I have not confessed all to my tormentors in the group. I have experienced nothing then. I have been with J. L. Moreno for a few days at his psychodrama retreat in Beacon, N.Y., and even preserve an absurd little certificate from that institution indicating my participation. Signed by the great Moreno himself, it is one of my most prized possessions, and I used to annoy the group enthusiasts at the Addiction Research Foundation by hanging it ostentatiously on the wall of my office there. It resembles one of those $25 doctorates obtainable from lots of such institutions of learning across the continent. Nothing. I have read the literature: that is the funniest defence of all. Who ever heard anyone claim legitimacy on the basis of so unnatural a thing as book learning? Certainly not anyone in the encounter movement today.

I have worked with numerous casualties of the encounter in my private practice of psychiatry. Again, nothing. Psychiatrists are fond of saying things like that. It only reveals that they are elitist, negative, suppressive of human potential, and generally lacking in awareness. They are desperate defenders of the Establishment and the myth of mental illness. They are afraid that a whole horde of real human beings are advancing into their territory with a view to actually helping people achieve joy and self-realization. Naturally the psychiatrists have tended to sniff a lot, whispering of qualifications and other irrelevant matters.

The problem is an ancient one. The Human Potential Movement has developed an ideological position, an array of techniques, and also a very useful defence against criticism. Anyone who is not a subscriber to the values of this new secular religion is not qualified to examine it. Yet it is famously true that the believers are either unwilling or unable to examine themselves.

The encounterists are very certain, for their part, that thousands of people have been entirely satisfied with their services. Nor can it be denied that great numbers of people claim they have benefited from Scientology, the encounter, LSD, the cadre schools of China, employment in the Mitsubishi works at Osaka, or any one of a thousand other happy entanglements devised by man for man. Testimonials abound, and these are commonly made by sincere and grateful people. It would seem, then, that any criticism of even the most irrational of approaches to either treatment, salvation or social stability is unwarranted. Many people have their desires satisfied and therefore the method, whatever it is, is an invention of great value.

Let us consider this argument. The dance trances of the Bushmen of the Kalahari Desert are inspiriting to individual participants and highly cohesive to the group as a whole. The Bushmen would probably argue, moreover, that their dance trances are more important to them than the wheel. For them, this ceremony is the most important social invention not of the century but of all time. What is the difference between a Bushman and an encounterist? Less than you might think. One difference, of course, is that of the two only the encounter leader would recognize the usefulness of this comparison and he alone would consider it, on reflection, a compliment. Living as he does in a static society, and lacking any knowledge of even the existence of so strong and wonderful a social invention as the encounter group, the Bushman would not be interested in the comparison at all.

Later in this book I will again refer to the trance and possession states that have been observed in every part of the world. For the moment I simply want to draw attention to the immodesty of the statements issued by our own shamans. These statements are songs of certainty. And that is what is so interesting about them. The utopian thinker always looks about him and sees that the world is not a perfect place. He muses accordingly on how he might improve it, and then he comes upon his invention. He recognizes that this idea is not only novel but also very wise. It is, in fact, The Answer.

The idea is then developed and presented to the world, sometimes with a singular lack of discretion. In due course a certain number of people are convinced that they have been saved. I am not inclined to argue with these people. I think it is splendid that they have achieved contentment, good health, joy, right-thinking citizenship, salvation, or anything else previously denied them. My argument is not with the converts but with the proselytizers. I must question their assumption that their technique is The Answer and that if only it could be applied universally there would be peace in the world or some other equally marvellous benefit for all mankind.

In fact the techniques I will be considering in this book are all designed to control behaviour, and achieve this end by bringing about the suspension of those mental processes that are essential for rational thought. The encounterists hold that the real man, the authentic man, is he who is feelingful and intuitive. Understanding, then, is something that comes to the believer through the agency of his passion and most emphatically not his intellect.

But men are famously gullible even before they are subjected to certain techniques that emphasize this tendency. Men are obedient and suggestible even when their judgment is not degraded by some interruption of the normal processes of their minds. And that is yet another matter I would particularly like to consider in this book. The shaman or medicine man probably does not have a very clear understanding of why his techniques are so effective. The evangelist is no doubt a good deal more sophisticated in this regard. The interrogator knows almost everything there is to know about the usefulness of alternating sensory deprivation and sensory bombardment, and about the unhinging value of fatigue, hunger, and mental and physical pain. The encounter leader is no less naive.

I will agree, then, that these techniques work. The history of the world has been largely determined by passionate and therefore uncritical adherence to beliefs and causes. Some of these have been benign and some unspeakably malignant. It is in this context that it will be useful to know something about the nature of the group movement and the techniques it employs, why they work, and on whom they are most liable to work. In short, everyone about to be involved either voluntarily or involuntarily in some variety of sensitivity training should know precisely what he is getting into. He should be aware of the possibility of certain defences even if he is disinclined to use them.

In particular, however, I have undertaken to write this book not for the person who is rushing eagerly into the arms of an encounterist but for the one who hesitates, concerned that the movement's excessive claims may not be valid in his own case. I will examine the hazards of sensitivity training then, and not unduly emphasize its benefits. I do this for two reasons. First, the joyous rewards of sensitivity training have been reported exhaustively over the last few years and there seems to me little need for any further rhapsodizing on this point. Secondly, I have a very particular appreciation of individuality, intelligence, dignity and privacy, and dislike anything that tends to threaten these things. As will be seen, the Human Potential Movement especially despises every one of the conditions I most profoundly appreciate. It emphasizes the necessity of experiencing unrestrained feeling in the immediate and glittering present and in so doing detaches itself from history on the one hand and from any intelligent consideration of the future on the other. It rejects learning. It is offended by the suggestion that in any population there will be vast individual differences. And it does all of these things even as it claims to represent the next step in the long process of the enlightenment of man and his society.

This last is the most intriguing of all the movement's presumptions. Of course the possibility that the encounter culture of William C. Schutz, or the third consciousness of Charles Reich, should actually represent a step in some agreeably upward direction, must be seen as an element in an ideological debate. Not everyone is convinced that this most recent revival of transcendentalist and utopian thought is any more valuable than were many quite similar visions in the past.

A few years ago I suggested that a government inquiry into the human potential movement and its indoctrination techniques might benefit a number of people. Such an inquiry was never instituted. This book, then, is a private inquiry. My intention is simply to note the uses and abuses of sensitivity training and a number of other techniques and practices that have either sprung from it or developed in parallel with it. All of these things are interesting, and some of them are even useful. Their most important aspect, however, is that they all contain certain tendencies that may be identified most clearly in every utopian tyranny that has ever come to my attention.

This is what is important to me. There is a fair amount of evidence by now that the human potential movement has reached its zenith. Whereas in the late 'sixties new human growth centres were opening all over the continent this trend has now been sharply checked. The rage for Organization Development in private corporations and branches of government has considerably subsided as well. The real problem is, however, as great as it ever was, and the spectacular but ephemeral success of the Human Potential Movement is an astounding illustration of it. It is certainly still useful to consider the T-group and its many successors because individual people are still being hurt by them, but my major interest is the extraordinary susceptibility of our population to every technique that offers personal fulfilment and enrichment of life, even though history abounds in virtually identical movements that turned out to be fraudulent in the extreme.

The recent decline of interest in the furious encounter does not signify that people have at last become rational and well protected against the charlatans who offer joy and creativity in six painless lessons or less. On the contrary, people are as vulnerable as they ever were. The techniques of persuasion that may be used against these people have now been refined to an unspeakable degree.

Also of great significance is the similarly powerful urge to transcend the self. This urge would seem to be very much in opposition to the need to conform, but it is possible to show that transcendence itself contains the possibility of utter betrayal of the self. He who has escaped from himself may, on that account, be rendered suggestible and easy prey to the strong influences around him. It is now well understood that these influences derive most persuasively and most economically from the group.

ANDREW MALCOLM

Toronto, Ontario
July, 1973

the
tyranny
of the group

1

The Will of the Group

Man lives in groups and the instinct to do so cannot be denied. He desires acceptance by the group and abhors rejection. In fact, affiliation is undoubtedly one of the strongest of needs. It is through association with other people that most human beings gratify their desires for affection and recognition. It is also through the constant interplay of ideas and feelings occurring in groups that people validate their social and philosophical positions.

Around the turn of the century Durkheim observed that when rural people were uprooted and thrown into swirling and unstable industrial societies they frequently experienced anomie, a condition in which there is a critical absence of core values. People must belong to groups with clearly-defined value systems because they cannot stand alone for very long. If they find themselves in a condition of normlessness and social isolation they become receptive to the call of any strong group that appears to offer them belongingness and hence security. In fact, whenever there has been rapid social change and instability, with large numbers of people deprived of their usual affiliations, the climate has been particularly receptive to the growth of rigid systems of belief, usually under the direction of strong and charismatic leaders. Contented people who know what their values are, and appreciate the institutions that uphold them, are usually quite resistant to the man who offers renewal and an exciting esprit de corps. A heroic revolutionary cause is inspiriting only to those convinced that their present social circumstances are profoundly lacking in value.

It is apparent, then, that group affiliation, and subjection to the values upheld by these groups, is necessary for almost everyone. It is every bit as apparent, however, that attachment to the group requires the individual to espouse certain common beliefs, values, and sentiments, if he is to support the group and be supported by it. In short, he must give up at least some of his individuality. He must conform. Should he fail to do this he will be regarded as deviant by the group, and face the threat of ostracism and a forcible return to that state of disequilibrium and loneliness that caused him to join the group in the first place. Groups are essential and ubiquitous, and they most certainly do have a tendency to command loyalty and obedience. It is not that this is necessarily evil. In fact, quite the opposite is usually the case. Unfortunately the group has a potential to produce blind loyalty, abject submission, and total obedience, and such conditions have invariably been dehumanizing in the end. Even so, for many of the people subjected to such pressures the experience is extremely revivifying and joyous, at least for a while. There is every reason to believe, for example, that during the period when the Third Reich was establishing its hegemony over most of Europe the majority of Germans were exhilarated and driven forward by a glorious vision of national and ethnic superiority. At the present time a similarly heroic submissiveness in the service of an exalted cause appears to guide the behaviour of the people of China.

Uniformity of opinion will tend to be stronger when the members of the group are particularly inclined to want to remain within it. That is to say, the more cohesive a group is, the more desire there will be to conform and encourage potentially deviant members to accept the group standards. If a group is less cohesive then it will be more vulnerable to fragmentation, and the pressures opposing such schism will be less specific and less powerful. On the other hand, the groups that condemn deviation most vigorously are those based on irrational beliefs and, for this reason, are especially cohesive. In such groups intense pressure will be brought to bear on the suspected deviant, but when every effort to recover the straying member fails, he is rejected with the same energy that was invested in the campaign for his salvation. His expulsion will be as vehement and passionate as the failed rescue mission.

We must also note that most people are members of several groups and that their loyalties to them will vary and sometimes even come into conflict. Since the essential function of group membership is to dispel a sense of personal disorientation, such conflict would eventually have to be resolved, a tendency that also produces greater simplicity in the life of the member. In a society characterized by diversity and individuality it is obviously comfortable to belong to a number of groups. If, however, a person should join an intensely cohesive and therefore satisfying group that is jealously exclusive as well, he will find it intolerably burdensome to maintain his membership in a number of other groups. Whether he has to withdraw from the other affiliations will of course depend on whether he is able to detect a conflict of values. The goals of the most persuasive group, as he perceives them or as they are revealed to him, cannot be denied if he is to be an authentic member. On joining the Nazi Party, a liberal and humanitarian person could not continue to associate with anyone identified as subhuman by the party. Nor must we imagine that previously liberal and humanitarian people were not attracted to this particular party. They were, and in great numbers, when they were persuaded that the greater goals of the party justified their allegiance to it. In that case their liberalism had to be redefined as a characteristic less relevant to the vital issues of the day than the objectives of National Socialism.

Paradoxically, membership in some groups has led to non-uniformity. In many encounter groups, for example, one of the group goals may be extreme toleration of eccentric patterns of behaviour. This is particularly liable to occur in any group in which an unusual thought or action is seen as innovative and hence creative. In fact, the manifestation of such novel and surprising behaviour is frequently taken as evidence of the group's success in releasing a member's repressed potential.

In such cases it may be observed that this is merely an expression of the same drive towards conformity noted in all groups. Here it is simply turned inside out. He who would be reserved and conservative is identified as deviant: he who would be explosive and unpredictable is identified as normative. In the latter case the principle of relevance requires that all members conform to the goal of public disinhibition. He who fails to express his gut-level feelings is regarded as deviant, and every effort will be made by the group to correct this regrettable indication of nonconformity.

Finally we may conclude that groups do encourage conformity but that this reductive tendency may be very supportive and necessary for individual well-being. Groups may be seen in this sense as serving a useful function in society. It is also true that the group can be used as an instrument of persuasion. This is the use that is of particular interest to my study. The group emphasizes the natural tendency to be suggestible and obedient.

Do you need any proof that man is suggestible? I would like to review briefly one of the earliest studies of the effects of group pressure on the distortion of judgment. In the late 'forties, Solomon Asch set up groups of seven or eight people and asked each to compare and match lines of different lengths. In every group there was one naive subject who was completely unaware that all the other members were stooges. The stooges were instructed always to give wrong answers, and this meant that the naive subject was presented with a conflict between the evidence of his senses and his desire not to be considered deviant by the group. About 13 of the 50 naive subjects held out doggedly throughout the entire series of 18 trials. They knew they were right, and the other seven people were inexplicably wrong. About a third of the subjects capitulated and agreed with the majority over half the time. All the other subjects were strung out on a line between these two defiant and submissive groups.

Asch felt that at least a few subjects were so influenced by the majority opinion that they actually perceived the majority estimates as being quite correct. In these cases there was no self-doubt, but rather a blind acceptance of the decision of the group. Most people who submitted, however, were aware that they perceived something other than what was reported by the majority, but concluded that their own perception must be at fault. In such a situation it seemed wise to take no chances. A third group of subjects perceived the lines correctly and knew that this was so. They submitted to the judgment of the majority solely so that they might not appear to be different.

In further studies Asch put two or more naive subjects with a group of instructed stooges. This resulted in a striking reduction in the amount of yielding. If, however, the second agreeing subject was also a stooge who subsequently changed his decision there was a full return of the amount of yielding. The remaining uninstructed subject was usually quite doubtful of his own judgment and strongly inclined to join the majority along with the previously supportive stooge. Moreover, if the majority opinions were wildly wrong rather than only minimally wrong this had only a very slight effect on the results of the trial.

Finally, when Asch put one subject who was instructed to make a wrong estimate with 16 naive subjects, all of whom tended to give correct estimates, there was much laughter concerning the odd judgment of this minority of one.

Now it may be argued that this was a very early and unsophisticated study. Very few conclusions concerning the nature and function of group norms can be made from it. Nor was the majority group of stooges really a group. It was an aggregate of subjects, a background of other people against whom the individual was briefly seen in relief.

These studies and others that have been carried out since that time do seem to illustrate, however, that for a variety of reasons the judgment and even the perception of the individual are affected by the group. If anything, the factor most obviously missing from such laboratory studies is feeling. There is no charismatic leader. There is no passionate cell of people exhorting the subject to make the majority decision in the interests of some political, therapeutic, or mystical cause. Nor does the subject know, love, or fear these bland ciphers who have simply been told to express unanimously erroneous judgments. There would be no intense emotional reason to trust the judgment of the majority and, more particularly, to be guided by it. It might not be incorrect to say that in such laboratory experiments the minimum amount of suggestibility would be elicited. The group in the real world would be far more persuasive.

Since the time of Solomon Asch, psychologists have intensified their pursuit of deception in the interests of science. Some experiments have been altogether reprehensible and have accordingly aroused very serious controversy regarding what constitutes an ethical standard for psychological research. It is regrettable, really, that at least a few of these deceptive studies have been of some value.

The work of Stanley Milgrim at Yale is a case in point. In the early 'sixties this social psychologist devised an ingenious method for the systematic measurement of obedience, and advertised in New Haven for subjects to participate in an educational experiment on the effects of punishment on memory. This study would pay $4.50 and last about an hour. The setting was an old house on High Street clearly marked as The Yale Interaction Laboratory. On entering this building the subject was met by a decent-looking chap in a lab coat who identified himself as the experimenter. The scientist then introduced the unsuspecting subject to a second man who, there was every reason to believe, was just another subject. This other man was about 50, a bit overweight, and evidently not in the best of health.

The experimenter explained to both men that the purpose of the Yale study was to discover a little more about the effects of negative reinforcement on learning. He pointed out that negative reinforcement occurred when a person was punished for getting something wrong. Positive reinforcement, which was not being tested, occurred when a person was rewarded for getting something right. The experimenter then said that one of the subjects was to be the "teacher" and the other was to be the "learner". These roles would be determined by drawing lots, he said. In fact the draw was rigged, and the real subject always became the teacher.

The learner, who was a stooge in the employ of the experimenter, was asked to step into an adjoining room where the real subject could see him being strapped into a device that resembled an electric chair. It was explained that the electrodes attached to his arms led to a shock generator in another room. Both men were then asked if they had any questions and the stooge said, very audibly, that two years ago he had had a mild heart condition diagnosed in a veteran's hospital. He wanted to know whether the experiment would be dangerous in that case, and was assured that it would not be.

The "teacher" was then taken to another room and seated before an elaborate console. There it was explained to him that there was a two-way intercom connecting him to the subject in the electric chair. He was to read a word and then a series of four additional words from a prepared list. The learner would then push one of four switches indicating his guess as to which of the four words was to be matched to the first one. If he got it right the teacher would simply go on to the second word series. If he got it wrong, the teacher was to push a switch that delivered an electric shock to the learner before proceeding to the next group of words and the next shock level.

The control board presented a series of 30 switches, each one clearly marked 15 volts, 30 volts, 45 volts and so on in 15-volt increments right up to 450. Each time a shock was administered an ominous buzzing sound was heard, and a prominent dial indicated a marked surge of power. To further emphasize the apparent reality of the situation the switches on the left were labelled "slight shock", those in the centre "intense shock", and those on the right, "danger: severe shock". The teacher was not told, of course, that Milgrim's real purpose was to discover at what shock level he would disobey and terminate the experiment.

Before the experiment began the teacher was himself given a decidedly unpleasant shock of what was described as 45 volts. Thus he knew the learner would definitely be reacting to pain. Work then got under way, and before long the learner would get something wrong. He was shocked according to the rules of the study; but his response would only be a mild "Ouch". With each successive punishment his response became more marked. At 135 volts he would shout to the effect that it really hurt. At 180 volts he said he could not endure this amount of pain. At 195 he said he was very worried about the heart condition that he had mentioned earlier. At 285 he emitted a fearful scream, and at 315 failed to answer. At this point the experimenter advised the teacher that after five seconds of silence he was to administer the next shock and proceed to the next word series. The interests of science required that the series be completed even though there was every reason to believe the learner had suffered a heart attack, and might even have died. Yale would take the responsibility and the teacher had nothing to worry about.

Now the learner's responses were all pre-recorded on tape and the electric shock generator, though it looked very impressive, was entirely phoney. The red lights indicating dangerous levels of shock and the darting shock energizer dial were all part of the deception. Nobody was being shocked at all, but the teacher had no way of knowing that this was so. He knew only that he was being paid to take part in an important educational experiment and that he had been instructed to follow the rules of the study and the orders of the experimenter in the lab coat.

The study was excruciatingly painful for a great many subjects and some finally told the experimenter that they could not go on. Even though science was to benefit from the work they still were unable to put a weak and severely ill man through such torture. Nevertheless, 65 per cent of the subjects proceeded to the bitter end, to the point of total silence, to the level of the apparently lethal 450 volts. And this was in New Haven.

Milgrim had originally conceived the idea of discovering why the Germans had been so obedient during the period of the Third Reich. He intended to carry out the study in Germany but in order to prepare for this work ran the pilot in New Haven. In the end, he decided that it was unnecessary to travel all the way to Germany. Americans appeared willing enough to co-operate with an established authority as long as they did not have to bear any responsibility for the dreadful results of their obedience.

Milgrim was still not quite satisfied. He wanted to know just how far he would have to go in order to bring about disobedience in a large number of people. Instead of having the learner in a remote room he brought him right into the same one with the teacher at the board. In this new situation, moreover, he did not strap the learner's arms to the chair. At the level of 150 volts the learner, still a stooge, lifted his arms from the electrodes and insisted that he must refuse to go on. The teacher was then instructed to take hold of the learner's hands and physically force them to the electrified plates so that the shock might be administered. In this vastly more intimate version of the study Milgrim still found that 30 per cent of the subjects were so obedient that they continued to the limit of the board with the learner in an apparent condition of cardiac arrest.

After the session each subject was told that the whole thing was a hoax. The man with the weak heart appeared, greeted everyone pleasantly, and the "teacher" was thanked for his co-operation. Science had nevertheless been greatly assisted, he was assured, and all was well. At the same time, many people have pointed out that such studies cause psychological harm to the subjects. Herbert Kelman of Harvard has observed: "At least some of the obedient subjects [in Milgrim's study] came away from the experience with lowered self-esteem, having to live with the realization that they were willing to yield to destructive authority to the point of inflicting extreme pain on a fellow human being".

It is not surprising that men are capable of great inhumanity or, for that matter, that they are supported in this behaviour by authority. Humans are extremely obedient, and we did not need Milgrim's study to establish that this is so. It could be argued, of course, that obedience is a very necessary quality in man. The civilized society could not long endure if people insisted on defying authority in every situation. In fact, the maintenance of any sort of social stability requires that individuals be obedient. This is all the greater reason, therefore, for protecting people from influences that make them set aside their capacity to be independent and humane. In every society the natural suggestibility and obedience of men are preyed upon by those who would increase their own influence and power. In a civilized society this is no less true, but the methods used will necessarily be more subtle and more glibly justified by reference to a greater good.

It is regrettable, therefore, that one of the most basic principles of today's Counter Culture is that individuality is the primary source of evil in Western society. In fact the only defence against the tendency to be obedient, so profoundly ingrained in man, is continuous encouragement of individual identity. When people are encouraged to diffuse their individuality instead, until it becomes continuous with the consciousness of the group, something is lost that has been our most vital defence against the oppressive rule of misguided authority.

Milgrim himself has tried to explain why people are so very obedient. He has observed that people are usually in such a state of autonomy as to be able to decide for themselves what they should do. In many situations, however, they switch into an entirely different state, a condition of agency. They no longer act for themselves; they act for someone else or on behalf of some ideological system. In this situation the agent does not feel responsible any longer for his own actions. The ruling authority assumes responsibility for all decision and action.

Now the real interest in all of this is that it seems altogether likely that this extraordinary state we may call "agency" is liable to supervene in circumstances of heightened suggestibility. Milgrim does not consider this matter, but it seems to me that when a person has come to suspend his rational judgment under the influence of a political demagogue, an evangelist, or an interrogator, he may be particularly vulnerable to switching into the role of agent. I would further suggest that intoxication with illusionogenic drugs would also serve to reduce the ordinary autonomy of the person and accordingly render him more vulnerable to this change in mental state. And finally, with particular reference to this study, I have little doubt that the specific reduction of individuality and intellect promoted in the encounter group tends also to lead to this same state. It may be useful to recall this question of agency in a later consideration of the fashionable introduction of sensitivity-training techniques into large organizations, both public and private. Once again, as we shall see, the members of such groups give up their right to be autonomous in favour of an apparently safer condition of agency.

Since Milgrim's work in the early 'sixties the flight into deception has been a particularly appealing one for a great many jaded psychologists. Sheridan and King decided that what was needed was a more authentic victim. They decided therefore to give the "learner" real shock, although some inexplicable surge of humanitarianism prevented them from using live human beings. Instead, they used a small dog and the shocks, progressively more powerful, elicited from this animal a series of responses. At first the dog flexed its foot in an attempt to withdraw from the uncomfortable stimulus. At higher levels he yelped and attempted to run away. At the highest level there was continuous howling and motor activity indicative of great and sustained agony.

These experimenters used 26 students enrolled in an introductory psychology class. The students were told that they had to participate in the study in order to satisfy a course requirement. As in the Milgrim study the subjects were told that the experiment was to test something other than their own willingness to disobey. Every time the puppy failed to give the right response the subject shocked him and watched him squirm and howl. Many of them protested and even wept as they pushed the switch for science; nevertheless over seventy-five per cent of the subjects proceeded to the highest level with the dog in constant turmoil and in full view. I think we need no further studies of this type.

It is certain that man is inclined to be obedient and that this is one reason why he has been successful as a social animal. Many thousands of years ago he survived by forming small nomadic bands for the purpose of hunting and gathering. Such groups have been identified in a variety of ways, but "primordial" or "tribal" are probably the most descriptive terms used. Morton Fried calls them egalitarian, because they, among all human associations, most completely approximate the ideal of primitive equality and simplicity. For these wandering people time and space are never clearly defined, and there is usually a mystical belief in the continuity of being. The style of such savages is especially appreciated by the disillusioned transcendentalists of our own age. They desire to return to what they conceive to be Eden before the Fall; but their failure to realize this blissful state, or at any rate to realize it for an extended period of time, is always the cause of their further disillusionment with life.

I am inclined to agree with the German sociologist Ferdinand Tönnies who pointed out in the late 1880s that there were two basic forms of human organization: a peasant group united by common ancestry or neighbourhood (the *gemeinschaft*), and a hierarchical arrangement which tended to be relatively impersonal (the *gesellschaft*).

Both forms of social organization have always existed side by side, but it is especially interesting to note that most people have insisted that the close and mutually supportive community has been the enemy of the grand bureaucracy and hence of authoritarianism. This is partly true, but there is something very deceptive about the statement. The small primordial group does not co-operate with the state when it exists in its simplest form, but it can be altered ingeniously to become the ideological primary group, and in this form a most powerful instrument for the control of deviant behaviour. In this regard it may be even more potent than the rigid hierarchical system which has always been identified as the basic cause of hopeless conformity. Every modern totalitarian state has systematically suppressed the intense and intimate folkish, kinship, and friendship groups, replacing them with groups whose values and behaviours were determined by the state.

The members of the primordial group tend to uphold the traditional order: the members of the ideological group advance the cause of the new order. This group is typically revolutionary and millenarian. It is impatient with the status quo and desires to sweep away every sign of the old order which is identified as suppressive and anti-human. The members of the ideological group are quite sure they have a corner on enlightenment, and that either God or Virtue is on their side.

It is the uprooted and dislocated members of folkish groups

who are especially liable to be excited by the slogans and claims of the sacred cause. Of course, not only the lonely and the dispossessed are vulnerable to the persuasive techniques of the revolution, but there seems to be no doubt that it is among them that the ideological group has always had the greatest appeal.

This was certainly the case only a few years ago in Germany. In fact the great Nazi rallies were perfect examples of the ideological group in the process of creation. I wonder whether those who say that the only person qualified to comment on the gut-level encounter is he who has himself experienced the gut-level encounter would also say that the only person qualified to comment on the significance of Nuremberg would be a Nazi storm trooper goose-stepping about under the klieg lights in the Zeppelinwiese. The Nuremberg rallies were masterpieces in the art of mass persuasion. Hundreds of thousands of people travelled in special trains from all over Germany to attend them. They were organized into rigidly-disciplined groups of athletes, women, storm troopers, armed forces, labour corps and Hitler youth, and they marched continuously beneath the torches, the banners and the searchlights, to the vast sounds of the massed bands and crowds singing "Deutschland" and shouting *Sieg Heil! Hitler, Vaterland!*

The pageantry and cameraderie picked up in intensity all week until on the last night, in the great hushed field, Hitler arrived and shouted through the microphone, "We are strong and will get stronger!" William Shirer wrote in his *Berlin Diary*: "And there, in the floodlit night, jammed together like sardines in one mass formation, the little men of Germany who have made Nazism possible achieved the highest state of being the Germanic man knows: the shedding of their individual souls and minds—with the personal responsibility and doubts and problems—until under the mystic lights and at the sound of the magic words of the Austrian, they were merged completely in the Germanic herd."

We will forgive Shirer for specifying the Germanic man in this account. He was observing 200,000 Nazi party officials experiencing unity and salvation, and it was an appalling spectacle. What we know is that the ancient Romans, the modern Americans, and every other mass of people were or are susceptible to precisely the same condition of helpless glorification through total submission to the experienced will of the assembly. It would not have been circumspect for a shopkeeper from Bonn to shout, "We want our leader! Nothing for us! Everything for England! Heil Churchill!" The tragedy of it is that probably very few shopkeepers from Bonn were resistant to the exalted state of mass consciousness being so brilliantly developed by Albert Speer and Julius Streicher. Germans believed passionately in the sanctity of their leaders because it was exciting to believe, and because their rationality had been systematically undermined. Dr. Goebbels was convinced that *Mein Kampf* showed a brilliant understanding of the value of propaganda. Commenting on this he said: "It would not be impossible to prove, with sufficient repetition and psychological understanding of the people concerned, that a square is in fact a circle. What, after all, are 'square' and 'circle'? They are mere words, and words can be moulded until they clothe ideas in disguise."

In the course of a very few years German citizens and soldiers came to act as agents of the state. They were therefore not personally responsible for their acts. Or so they believed. There is, in all men, this dreadful kamikaze urge, but if the self is to be submerged, into what must it sink? It must always be immersed in the consciousness of the group. Every man is inclined to be obedient. He desires further to conform to the values of some group he perceives as strong and influential. If this group emphasizes the value of raw emotion and the rejection of identity and intellect then he will soon experience heightened suggestibility. Closure will occur around any remaining ideas he might previously have found distasteful. Then, purified and confident, he will begin to act, not for himself, but for the group. In

Germany, of course, the deviant person could expect to be seized in the night and transported to a concentration camp. In America he who dissents from the cultural patterns of his neighbourhood or the policies of his company can expect to be dealt with rather less severely. Our groups are persuasive, but they are not supported by the ultimate methods of coercion.

2
Transcendence

So far I have been dealing with the desire to abandon one's self in the greater consciousness of the group. To be an individual in a complex and bewildering world is very difficult. Sensing their smallness and relative helplessness, many people are strongly inclined to submerge themselves in what they perceive to be the vastly more powerful identity of the group. In so doing they may sacrifice their independence but they gain something else that can only be recognized as power. Alone, they are weak: together, they are a force that commands respect. And they are uplifted because they know they are a part of this great force. The organizers of the movement, who are often capable of some degree of cynicism, do not explain that every man is expendable. On the contrary, they emphasize the high-spirited individuality of every member of the mass.

There is this strong association, then, between the act of submission and the reward of personal significance. We will come upon this paradox again and again in the study of the group experience. Hapless man, longing always for a richer experience, for fulfilment, for self-realization, is tempted to achieve these things by restraining those functions of his mind on which his individuality must ultimately depend.

It is very clear that men in diverse places and times have expressed a desire to achieve transcendence. That is to say they have grown tired of their apathy and ordinariness and they have sought to alter their states of consciousness in such a way as to become, at least temporarily, quite unlike themselves. Usually the experience of the altered state of consciousness (A.S.C.) is temporary; but because a person in such a condition is highly suggestible, the learning that takes place in the course of this experience persists beyond the period of the exaltation.

An A.S.C. is a condition of the mind that deviates from that which is experienced by a person in a state of alert waking consciousness. According to Arnold Ludwig: "This sufficient deviation may be represented by a great preoccupation with internal sensations or mental processes than is usual, by changes in the formal characteristics of thought, and by impairment of reality testing to various degrees."

The circumstances under which the A.S.C. appears may be classified under three general headings which we may call sensory bombardment, sensory deprivation, and physiological abnormalities. It would seem that normal consciousness can be maintained only when the inflow of stimuli from either the outside world or the body itself is confined to an optimal level. In the living organism equilibrium is always essential. Any influence that persistently unbalances body function will result in the appearance of abnormal physical and mental states. The altered state of consciousness is an example of mental disequilibrium and is important to us because it is when a person is in this state that he is peculiarly vulnerable to the loss of his individuality.

When someone is subjected to excessive sensory stimulation, and particularly when this is accompanied by intense emotional and physical activity, the optimal level at which normal consciousness can be maintained may be exceeded, and the A.S.C.

may supervene. Thus in dance trances and possession states, religious revivalism, brainwashing and many other circumstances in which high emotion is associated with physical activity and sensory overstimulation it is not unusual for people to depart, however briefly, from normal waking consciousness.

An extraordinary example of sensory bombardment in association with intense group pressure is offered by the spirit-possession cult of Haiti. In the voodoo religion it is understood that illness is due either to personal sin or to the influence of someone who has evil designs on the afflicted person. The only way one can recover is to participate in a voodoo ceremony and become possessed by one of the many *loa* or spirits that are the deities of this folk religion. Furthermore, since illness is felt to indicate that the sufferer has broken a taboo the need to become possessed is a very urgent one. If he should fail to become entranced and then possessed by a god he runs the grave risk of being ostracized by his fellow believers. Everything is done, accordingly, to bring the participant to such a state of otherworldliness as to make him receptive to the entry of the loa. The person possessed is then described as a *cheval,* which is the French word for horse, and it is felt that his soul has been perfectly mounted by the god. In this circumstance all of the cheval's ideas and acts are due entirely to the loa. The person now acts as an agent of the voodoo cult.

In order to bring about this extraordinary condition the room is filled with the famous driving rhythm of the voodoo drums. In referring to the power of the drums, Aldous Huxley suggested that a group of the most rational of our philosophers should be shut up in a hot room full of Moroccan Dervishes or Haitian voodooists. He insisted that these learned gentlemen would not long retain their critical and self-conscious personalities. He said: "If exposed long enough to the tom-toms and the singing every one of our philosophers would end up capering and howling with the savages."

The error in this is that it is not only the drums that bring about the altered state of consciousness. The whole atmosphere is charged with emotion. Drugs of various kinds, vigorous dancing and participation in a series of magical religious ceremonies, all contribute to the impact on the brain. Many of the participants fast before the ceremony, and extended prayer is usual. The excitement during the ceremony is highly contagious as one person after another is mounted by a loa and caused to behave as though he were bewitched. Ari Kiev has written: "It is clear that during ceremonies an individual's sense of self-identity and self-awareness is reduced and that a sense of merging with the group is increased by the emotionally aroused atmosphere, with the group singing and clapping in unison to the ministrations of the *hungan."*

We must remember that the sufferer desperately wants to be possessed. Not to achieve this exalted state is to be rejected by the gods and hence by the group. The participant must show he is unhesitatingly a member of the cult, and the only way he can prove the completeness of his belief is to be chosen by a loa as a worthy mount. Kiev goes on: "This necessitates his adopting a passive role which in turn makes him more amenable to suggestion by the healer. The hungan's power and omnipotence, coupled with the group pressure to conform, are especially influential on those who resist adopting this role." It is essential that the participant give himself up entirely. Any resistance brings forth redoubled effort on the part of the hungan and the other dancers until, finally, there is total collapse. He who must have violated a taboo ceases to exist, the loa rides joyously in his head, and his rebirth is assured.

Later we shall see how astonishingly similar this ceremony is to the more lively varieties of the encounter. For the moment I want to note that in circumstances in which there is intense sensory overstimulation the human brain can lose its capacity to test reality and be rendered, therefore, vulnerable to suggestion. The voodoo cult, it should also be said, is an extremely stabilizing institution in Haiti. It is constantly available and believed in implicitly. It is a very complex religious system that comprises gods, angels, sacred rites, churches, a clergy, and historical connections to both African folk religions and Roman Catholicism. Voodoo functions as a cohesive force among the people of Haiti. Precisely the opposite must be said of the human potential movement in Western society today. Although spirit possession is rare in North America the A.S.C., and particularly the states of mind that lead up to it, certainly is not. Panic and rage reactions, and trance states associated with emotional contagion and group regression, are quite common here. I recall quite vividly three dissimilar rituals in which either trance or a condition approximating it was observed by me to occur in large numbers of people participating in a public event.

The first was a religious revival meeting in San Antonio in which the entire programme was arranged by the evangelist with the most exquisite appreciation of the consecutive stages of emotional arousal. The hall was very large, and filled nearly to capacity. The lights grew dimmer and the organ more powerful as the evening went on. The event began with a series of assistant evangelists warming up the crowd with straight-from-the-shoulder information regarding the existence of sin and the wrath of God. Various groups of singers in the employ of the organization entertained the congregation with decidedly rhythmical songs and participation was strongly encouraged. Testimonials came from supplicants who were said to have attended the crusade on previous nights. Blind people had seen, crippled people had walked, and deathly ill people had not died.

Finally the leader strode to centre stage and proceeded to harangue the audience in the most gravelly of voices for at least an hour. He was a specialist in the art of the dread pause, the rhetorical question, the exhortation to respond, and the dramatic anecdote. His message was rock-hard Biblical simplicity and he was appalled by sin of every possible description. The audience sang for him, clapped for him, stood for him, and sat for him. Excitement in the hall was very active and intense. He instructed his people to stand for at least the tenth time. He then told them to put their left hand over that part of their body that was ailing and to extend their right hand to God.

I was not present at Nuremberg when a hundred thousand people gave the straight-arm Nazi salute to the Führer. I have only been in San Antonio when a thousand straight-armed hands stretched imploringly toward the evangelist in the spotlight on the stage. The effect was electrifying. People began to swoon all over the auditorium, and everywhere assistants had been placed to catch those people overcome with the spirit of the Lord. A strange and constant wailing now began and continued without interruption until the end of the service. People were exhorted to move to the front and rise up to the stage. Soon there was a long line of shabbily-dressed people hoping once again for the miracle that had eluded them.

They believed this time they would be healed and saved. The evangelist hurled forth the charge that the people were not yet ready to meet their Maker. "Are you saved? Are you saved? What would happen to you if you left this hall and were suddenly killed and then you heard the trumpets of heaven?" From the balcony a hidden chorus of three heavenly trumpeters shocked the hall with an ominous fanfare. And so the evening ended with the most terrible doubt in the shattered minds of hundreds of people. A great many, of course, did not care to run the risk. They were overwhelmed, and in this condition made a decision for Christ before they left the hall.

The second of my examples is a professional hockey match in which the righteous Toronto Maple Leafs were being humiliated by a band of alien maulers representing the Boston Bruins. In that case the fans were enthralled by every outburst of action and particularly every evidence of blood-lust in defence of their beloved Leafs. The roars were overwhelming and extraordinarily well synchronized. At various moments in the contest the crowd seemed to function as a single unit, a mob, unrestrained and greedy for nothing short of massacre. Some members of the audience became quite glassy-eyed and on the edge of ecstasy immediately after a spirited power play resulted in a necessary, though not quite equalizing, goal. I saw at that time that a mob undoubtedly develops a personality which is more than an aggregation of all the individuals comprising it.

The mob has a capacity to simplify the issues and perfectly, if irrationally, identify the one true enemy. I was never in the Colosseum at Rome when gladiators were thrown in to battle to the death for the amusement of the people. But I felt that if the crowd at Maple Leaf Gardens had been asked to turn their collective thumbs up or down to determine whether or not a brutish defenceman from Boston should be speared on the spot, many would not have spared him. The surrounding culture, however, did not allow decisions to be made in that way. The referee simply intervened and sent the offender to the penalty box. He was hissed at all the way to the box, and the rink was soon covered with debris. The whole performance was no less barbaric than anything that happened in the Colosseum except for the fact that the defenceman was not actually murdered. When he returned to the ice, however, three broad-backed Leafs soon managed to spin him into the boards with such force as to require his withdrawal from the game. One of these avengers was penalized in turn, and advanced to the box amid the cheers of the crowd. The referee, on the other hand, was identified as a subversive.

Again we see that high emotion is contagious, and particularly so when it occurs in association with deafening sound and a common purpose. Camp meetings and professional hockey games are particularly devoid of intellectual content for the majority of participants. And so, most importantly, are great rallies of a specifically political nature.

My third example is again secular, but that does not mean that it was lacking in either passion or irrational behaviour. I had heard a great deal about the unrestrained emotion that was regularly expressed at the huge concerts staged by the Beatles during their first American tour. The reality of the event was far more extraordinary than any account of it that I had read. The great auditorium was quite dark and yet it glittered from the thousands of flash-bulbs that burst irregularly in every quarter. The crowd shrieked continuously in such a curious fashion that there seemed to be an unending high-pitched whistle obliterating entirely any sound that may have proceeded from the stage. This eerie sound began before the idols appeared and continued until long after they had swept from the hall. Everywhere there were people in ecstatic and frequently orgasmic states. They engaged in apparently purposeless, convulsive movements of their arms and legs, all the time emitting this astounding shriek that had little to do with what might be called music appreciation.

The crowd was unhinged, transported, and utterly irrational. Again, however, there were no organizing instructions from the stage. The crowd had been brought to a point at which many of its members were clearly experiencing an altered state of consciousness, but no suggestions were made to them that might have determined their subsequent behaviour. This was in the mid-'sixties and therefore rock concerts were not yet delivering the message that everyone should tune in, turn on, and drop out. This was still the period of naive innocence in which the Beatles were playing, "I Wanna Hold Your Hand." "Strawberry Fields Forever" and "Lucy in the Sky with Diamonds" came much later.

The examples I have given up to now have all been illustrations of excessive sensory stimulation of the brain. It is important for us to realize, however, that the A.S.C. may also appear when there is a marked reduction of sensory stimulation and motor activity.

It would seem that the profound mental changes occurring in the course of passive meditation are due, at least in part, to sensory under-stimulation. Such mystical or revelatory states as nirvana, cosmic consciousness and samadhi occur on this basis.

It has been known for some time that people in solitary confinement show mental disturbances largely because they are denied the opportunity to validate their experiences with other people, but also because sound, light, and movement are greatly reduced. Similarly, people have experienced the A.S.C. in the tank respirators used in the treatment of serious cases of polio. By now a great deal of experimental work on the effects of sensory deprivation has been carried out. Usually the subject has been suspended in a water tank in absolute darkness and silence. Most people in this situation will develop a most abnormal state of mind. They will hallucinate and experience a strange dreamlike condition which may be pleasureable but may more often be nightmarish. One of the early workers in this field, D. C. Hebb, has stated that sensory deprivation is so deranging to a person that it "can disturb his capacity for critical judgment, making him eager to listen to and believe any sort of preposterous nonsense."

And this brings me to the remarkable case of Dr. John Lilly, an eminent scientist whose search for enlightenment has been lifelong and perilous. Lilly began life as a Catholic but quite early rejected this faith. He studied physics, biology, and eventually medicine. He then specialized in neurophysiology, while at the same time undergoing a training analysis to qualify as a psychoanalyst. In 1954, he became interested in the work being done in sensory deprivation and began to immerse himself in his private tank. Of course he regularly experienced the A.S.C. but his conclusions, interestingly, were not that his mind had been made to malfunction. Instead, he saw that this induced aberration was evidence of mental expansion. He then began to wonder what it must be like to be a dolphin, an animal with a brain even larger than that of man, who spends his entire life suspended in water. To find the answer to this question, Lilly established the Communications Research Institute in the Virgin Islands, and in 1959 began his famous attempt to make contact with these undoubtedly intelligent mammals. He was not successful, but after a number of years decided that since dolphins were just as sensitive as man he had no right to keep them in captivity. He reached this conclusion in 1964, while on an LSD trip in his personal tank. The dolphins were in other tanks in the same laboratory and Lilly could sense their predicament. In his own condition of physical isolation and under the influence of acid he saw for the first time the ethical implications of his beliefs about dolphins. In the next two weeks six of his dolphins committed suicide by, he claimed, simply ceasing to breathe. Although he had kept the dolphins for up to seven years he was convinced that this proved the truth of his conclusions, and he released his remaining three immediately.

Lilly's use of LSD provides a convenient bridge between sensory deprivation and a third important group of variations that can bring about the A.S.C. It has been known for a very long time that excessive changes in body chemistry can result in aberrant mental states. Very low and very high blood sugar, abnormal carbon dioxide and oxygen ratios (in breathholding and hyper-ventilation), dehydration, as well as many kinds of hormonal imbalance, can produce profound changes in consciousness. Withdrawal from certain drugs after a person has become physiologically dependent on them can also produce the A.S.C. Delirium tremens in the course of alcohol withdrawal is an outstanding example of this effect.

However the administration of a great variety of chemicals, particularly such illusionogens as marijuana and LSD, will also result in the A.S.C. It was on the basis of this observation that I developed a few years ago, a hypothesis that the use of certain drugs might be one of several factors in the causation of attitudinal change, and that this might be related to the observed diffusion of social alienation in Western society. The essential idea of this hypothesis is that there are three variables determining the social and psychological effects of the illusionogens. These are the personality of the subject, the pharmacological properties of the drug, and the nature of the milieu in which the drug is taken. Thus a person who is naive and easily persuaded will, on taking a sufficient amount of LSD, soon find himself quite dependent on the support of some strong person in his milieu. In this way he might come to subscribe uncritically to an entirely new system of values. He might, in effect, be converted, and this new system of belief would become more certainly fixed in his mind with each repetition of the drug experience.

We must remember that the aberrant state of mind known as the altered state of consciousness can also develop in circumstances in which no drug whatsoever is used. Moreover the tendency to be suggestible does not depend on the ultimate achievement of the A.S.C. Indeed there are numerous techniques that tend to suspend rational thinking and create, as a consequence, a condition of heightened suggestibility. I have observed that in those techniques that do not depend on the use of intoxicating chemicals there is a common tendency to promote alternating states of sensory overstimulation and sensory deprivation, emotional contagion, and group regression. The result is an enhancement of the tendency, seen in all people, to be obedient and suggestible.

Experts in the techniques of persuasion rarely rely on only one of these methods. They use several of them in combination because they know that this will result in an additive effect. In any case drug-free mysticism, drug intoxication, and the immersion of the self in the group have, in themselves, many common characteristics. The most important of these is that they all depend on regression to a lower level of mental organization than that which is known as normal waking consciousness.

The human mind survived and evolved through the making of conscious transactions with reality. Yet man has constantly shown the strongest urge to escape from the limitations of consciousness. In some cases—voodoo is an example—this is because he has conceived of the gods as being so vast in power and intelligence as to be beyond the reach of ordinary men. Only he who is entranced can be possessed; and only he who is possessed can be saved. It is an ancient belief occurring in a variety of forms all over the earth. Sometimes special people—shamans, medicine men and priests—have been appointed to communicate with the gods. More often the entire group has been led by these great teachers to achieve transcendence and hence enlightenment. The teaching, however, has never been that the members of the flock should think. On the contrary it has always been that they should feel. And so it is today as it has always been. In the modern industrial state we again see the emergence in very large numbers of people of the desire to experience the transcendental state. It would be naive to identify this urge as the evolution of Consciousness III, or the sudden appearance in our midst of *Homo transcendentia*.

According to John Lilly, the effects of sensory deprivation are very similar to those of LSD. The only difference, according to him, is that with LSD the mental and spiritual energy is enormously increased. This makes transcendence that much easier. In Lilly's case just floating around in the water tank was sufficient to enable him to tune in on a network of communication from other civilizations. In fact he said he was able to learn how to park his body and travel to various places around the world and, finally, around the galaxy. With LSD, Lilly began to see himself more and more as an adventurer. His critics suggested that what he was experiencing was temporary psychosis but he responded quite simply with the observation that his critics were conceptually limited. He said: "I think the attempt to define all mystical, transcendental and ecstatic experiences which do not fit in with the categories of consensus reality as psychotic is conceptually limiting and comes from a timidity which is not seemly for the honest, open-minded explorer."

Given such an orientation it is not surprising that Lilly eventually found himself very much in harmony with the prophets of the human potential movement. In 1969, he became a resident and teacher at Esalen, the famous human growth centre that will be described later in this book. As might have been predicted, however, the encounter and all the other exotic diversions of Esalen were not sufficiently satisfying. Always on the lookout for any new means to achieve enlightenment Lilly heard of the work of the great Bolivian master Oscar Ichazo. This sage taught an up-dated version of the Persian Sufi method for achieving the A.S.C., and in 1971 Lilly travelled all the way to Arica in Chile where Ichazo had established a school. It is interesting that of the fifty original seekers who made the trip to Chile almost half were defectors from Esalen. They each paid up to $7,000 for the ten-month experience. Forty-two of the graduates founded the Arica Institute in America, Inc., and were soon establishing branches in a dozen North American cities.

Arica is an incredible mixture of Hinduism, Sufism, Tibetan Lamaism, Zen Buddhism and American human potentialism. Arica itself may soon fade away, but this contemporary tendency to create unholy amalgams of a dozen different spiritual sources will reappear in different forms for many years to come. Ichazo mixed up African dances, Egyptian gymnastics, and bits of most of the mystery religions that have left any record of their beliefs and rituals. His proclaimed goal became nothing less than total enlightenment and serenity. One of his exercises is the "Audicon Plantar." It is designed to improve the hearing in the feet. The supplicants are advised to listen to the sound source through their soles. The students may then be required to concentrate their attention on various parts of the body for strictly determined periods of time. Thus they may consider their large intestines for eight minutes and 40 seconds. This attention to detail gives a clear impression of vast knowledge, however arcane it may be. One of the most intriguing exercises is called "Passive in the Cosmos." In this the student holds one arm straight up from the shoulder and in this way feels himself absorbing the vibrations of the solar system and beyond. I am immediately reminded of the instructions of the evangelist in San Antonio and I can easily imagine a large group of Arica believers making their straight-arm salute to the cosmos.

In fact it is numerical razzle-dazzle that is one of the essential characteristics of Arica training. Ichazo holds that level 48 is the rational neutral state. This would correspond to what I have previously called normal waking consciousness. However he who would achieve transcendence must engage in the many exercises and group functions of Arica. He may then be rewarded with the nirvana of level 24. This is what is called satori or enlightenment, but it is only the merest entry into this state. At level 24 the student is able to do some activity well and without conflict. It is the state of professional satori.

York University in Toronto, by virtue of its intense involvement in the encounter culture, soon became a most receptive environment for the seeding of Ichazo's method. In early 1973 York offered a course in Arica training. The university published a statement to the effect that "Arica training offers a system of human development carefully structured to produce lucid thought, emotional balance, serenity and joy. The result is the total integration of mind, emotion and body. A partial list of subjects studied in The Training are: meditation, mantram, creative movement, mentation, kundalini yoga, study of various levels of consciousness up to 'basic satori' or 'permanent 24'."

Ichazo offers more. At level 12 the student achieves a condition of blissful awareness. I am reminded here of the claim of the followers of Maharaj Ji that once they are "given knowledge" they consider themselves to be blissed out. The followers of this youthful guru are, like Ichazo's devotees, bewildered defectors from the encounter movement, the psychedelic drug culture, or both—usually both. According to John Lilly, level 12 closely resembles the beginning of a good LSD trip. The student can no longer function in the world and often cannot speak. He lives entirely in the here and now, and this is precisely where the encounter leaders say we should all live at all times.

At level 6 the student steps out of his body for the first time. This appears to resemble what the extrasensory perception people call astral projection. Lilly claims that at level 6 the student becomes a point of consciousness. This point is highly mobile and thus it may move in and out of the body. This is still not all. At level 3, the highest level of satori from which it is possible to return to the body, the devotee becomes a part of a surface that extends throughout the universe. This, presumably, is what R. M. Bucke described as cosmic consciousness. It is Buddhahood, total mystical union with all men, all nature, and the entire cosmos. According to Lilly: "It was in this state that I experienced 'myself' as melded and intertwined with hundreds of billions of other beings in a thin sheet of consciousness that is distributed around the galaxy."

It is not entirely clear how Lilly achieved this memorable condition but we may be certain he used a variety of techniques designed to interrupt the balancing processes of the brain. For many people it is exhilarating to suspend rational thought. In fact the essential ideological conflict we are experiencing today has been discussed for thousands of years. This conflict, as H. G. Levitch has pointed out, is exemplified by the nearly polar positions of Goethe and Blake. Goethe saw man as an organic structure not dissimilar to a tree. The tree starts its existence as a seed; it draws sustenance from nature and grows; it enlarges itself by adding to its outreach and also to its girth; and finally it dies. When this happens the tree disintegrates, and is soon replaced by an equally mortal tree. For Goethe, then, it is the nature of man to try to become more mature through experience. Levitch observes: "If there is to be an 'end', it is the biological death of the organism. Thus the 'means' itself is all that matters. For Goethe, the alternative to activity is stagnation and inertia; and that stagnation and inertia is death to the man."

It is apparent that this view of man is the dominant one in modern society. It is secular and rational and utterly lacking in illusion. A modern poet, George Jonas, puts it this way:

"I met God yesterday.
He sat on a sort of throne
We were both slightly embarrassed.
'I have no answers for you,' he said finally.
I was relieved but tried not to show it.
I had no questions."

The position of William Blake is very different. For Blake it is only through the recognition of the Infinite in all things that Freedom can be attained. Levitch continues: "Man begins Whole; he is fragmented by his Fall into Disunity; he awakens to an Awareness of his False Consciousness and Selfhood; and he is energized to pursue his obsessive Will to Unity and Reintegration with the Infinite."

The world called real is, for Blake, irrational, but there is a divine plan that must be sought by all who would achieve tranquillity. Levitch says: "What is then aspired to is a kind of implosive, traumatic experience which will put the fragmented man back together again, re-achieve a kind of transcendental, non-corporeal existence which is divine innocence—the stable, inactive, whole oneness." It is this belief in the possibility of transcendence that has caused people to dance to the voodoo drums, sink before the hands of the evangelists, float in the dark experimental tanks, swallow LSD, grasp each other in encounter groups and travel all over the world to sit at the feet of each new master of the art of enlightenment.

3

Behaviour Control

While the French of the 18th Century were speculating on the nature of the ideal egalitarian state, the English were being led to regard their spiritual salvation as something vastly more important than their earthly well-being.

The British Methodist revival was contemporaneous with the Age of Reason in France. John Wesley was arousing high passion and urgent desire for conversion on the part of many thousands of people. He did this by describing the horrors of damnation in great detail. Eternal agony engulfed in fire and brimstone was the certain fate of anyone so wretched as to leave the meeting without making a decision. It was not safe to be unsaved. Any sudden accident might deprive the person of his life and then, if he was not in a state of grace, he would be swept helplessly down to the pits of hell. The only defence against this awful fate was to change utterly, and change, for Wesley, was total acceptance of the Methodist creed.

The real interest in the Wesleyan phenomenon, however, is in the institution known as The Class. Wesley and his followers knew very well that a sudden conversion, however desirable it might be, had a tendency to be short-lived. It was almost two hundred years later before Pavlov discovered the necessity of reinforcement for a conditioned reflex to be maintained. By instituting The Class, Wesley anticipated Pavlov and the modern interrogators. His converts were gathered into small groups of about ten people and these groups were instructed to meet at least once a week under the direction of an appointed leader. At these meetings were discussed any difficulties that had blocked the convert's success in achieving sanctification. Problems relating to the future life of the repentant sinner were also reviewed within the group. In this way, as Wesley put it: "Evil men were detected and reproved. If they forsook their sin, we received them gladly; if they obstinately persisted therein it was openly declared that they were not of us."

In 18th-century England it was very difficult for any member of a Class to defy the absolute authority of the Group. Lonely defiance was mad, absurd, when all other members agreed that repentance was the *sine qua non* of salvation, and that the punishment for the failure to take this step was ghastly in the extreme. William Sargant concludes an interesting discussion of the Wesleyan system: "The Class meetings were intended for those already sensitized by their sudden and overwhelming conversion experiences; the close group feeling, the communal hymns and prayers, the intimate discussion of personal problems and advice on ways of avoiding 'the wrath to come' were a constant reminder of their original sanctification."

The ministry of John Wesley and the other English Methodists was strongly anti-revolutionary. People were directed to the dread problem of eternity and not the immediately obvious problem of a poverty- and disease-stricken present. On the other side of the Channel the French were moving inexorably towards the cataclysm of 1789. The philosophes were concerned to save man exactly where he stood on earth, and proposed, with increasing urgency, that this work be undertaken immediately. In the end, however, the French Revolution became every bit as passionate as was the Methodist Revival. In fact the revolution was ultimately as irrational as the hundreds of utopian movements that had developed in Europe over many centuries. Chiliasm, or the belief that Christ will return to earth to rule during the millennium, had often been seen before the 18th Century. Such movements differed in one basic respect from that of the Enlightenment, and this was in their invariable tendency to create a society in which men would be able to face God directly, without the interference of intermediary powers either spiritual or temporal. Otherwise they were all very similar. A society of men would be created in which every individual would be completely free and completely equal, and yet they would all act as one, and in perfect accord. In a few cases—the Anabaptists of Münster and the Calvinists of Geneva are two examples—force was finally used to create the uniformity that was God's will. In the case of 18th-century France, Messianism was based not on the absolute supremacy of God but rather on the absolute supremacy of man's reason. Happiness on earth was to come about through the radical transformation of society in accordance with what was called the natural order.

For these philosophes man was inherently good: it was his institutions that were evil. These institutions thwarted man, blocked his aspirations and corrupted him; but all the time man's real interest was the general social good. Holbach held that if men were frustrated, rent by passions, and confused by a variety of urges, then they would be unhappy. The only truly happy man was he who realized that his contentment depended entirely on his adjustment to the natural order of things. In such a case he would pursue happiness in perfect harmony with his fellow men. However, this excellent harmony was not something that would arise in society without careful planning. If the design of nature was to be realized, a legislator had to offer his services to man. Helvétius, one of the great philosophes of the 18th Century, observed that it was for the legislator to discover means of putting men under the necessity of being virtuous. He then went on to say that this could be best achieved by creating certain new and entirely rational institutions and laws, and by providing the people with not only an enlightening education but also a proper system of rewards and punishments. Men are virtuous, then, but certain restraints are necessary if this excellent characteristic is to be fully manifested.

Commenting on the evolution of totalitarian democracy in 18th-century France, Talman has written: "The very idea of a self-contained system from which all evil and unhappiness have been exorcised is totalitarian. The assumption that such a scheme of things is feasible and indeed inevitable is an invitation to a regime to proclaim that it embodies this perfection, to exact from its citizens recognition and submission and to brand opposition as vice and perversion."

It follows from this that if a man should lack a proper awareness of his own natural virtue then he is in need of re-education. And this principle, which was given its first practical demonstration by the Jacobins of 18th-century France, has remained the basic difference between liberal and totalitarian democracy to this day. The former proceeds by trial and error; the latter, founded as it is on some immutable truth concerning the perfectibility of man, proceeds by coercion and the exclusion of the deviant individual from the collectivity. The most intriguing and at the same time appalling aspect of such utopian systems of thought is that they affirm their interest in freedom and the rights of man even as they systematically simplify society, suppress individual freedom of thought and action, and debase the meaning of human dignity.

Yet these thinkers who first enunciated the principle of the natural order did not conceive of the use of force to bring about their ideal society. They actually believed that in the perfect system there would be no need to restrict free expression in any way. As Talman puts it: "Opposition to the natural order would be unthinkable except from fools or perverted individuals."

The philosophes may have been very naive but they were not

fools. There were still fools in France, however, and these were preyed upon in the 18th Century in a manner that can hardly be distinguished from how their descendants are preyed upon today. During the period when the philosophes were innocently creating totalitarian democracy a famous healer conducted sessions in which his clients would sit gripping thumbs around a large wooden tub. Jointed rods extended from this tub to touch the various afflicted parts of the clients. The great man walked about this circle dressed in a lilac suit, carrying a metal wand, and playing music on a harmonica. In the course of the many hours of the session he would occasionally touch one of his clients with his magic wand and the universal fluid would flow from the tub to the body of the sufferer. The tension in the room was also electric and there was much screaming, weeping, uncontrolled laughter and even, in some cases, convulsions.

The healer was Antoine Mesmer and his experiment with animal magnetism occurred in 1784. In the 'seventies of our own century some practitioners of the new mind quackery have revived Mesmer's spirit and indeed have come close to duplicating his very techniques. In fact today we may observe a surging revival of irrational neo-romanticism. We may discern many signs of a new movement that is a direct descendant of the Christian radicalism of the Middle Ages, the secular radicalism of the French Revolution, and the charlatanism of all times. This modern revival, however, is marked by a philosophical reversion to the extreme anti-intellectualism of the Christians even though it is man, and not God, who has been deified. Locke and Rousseau worshipped man, but it was his reason that they admired and eventually reason was enthroned at Paris. The members of the encounter culture of today reject both God and reason and they proceed directly to the very source of elemental passion that in the end ruined both Anabaptists and France's revolutionaries.

The human potential movement often refers to the need for an increased understanding of personal and social change, to the humane management of change, and to enlightened re-education. Textbooks on sociology, on the other hand, refer rather more bluntly to adult resocialization.

Of course people modify their attitudes, behaviour, and the way in which they see themselves, continuously throughout life. New experiences lead to new roles, and in turn these engender new experiences. Sociologists define such gradual change as continuing socialization. The term resocialization refers to change that is both rapid and profound. It may involve the complete abandonment of one's way of life and the adoption of another that is actually incompatible with the former. In such cases as religious conversion, brainwashing, and the intensive reconditioning of, for example, sex offenders, the result of resocialization is intended to be renunciation of the past and total acceptance of completely new values and modes of behaviour.

An interesting example of an attempt to cause very rapid resocialization is that of R.O.A.R.E. (Re-Education of Attitudes and Repressed Emotion), a form of encounter therapy that has been used at the Rahway Treatment Unit for the treatment of sex offenders incarcerated in the New Jersey prison system. R.O.A.R.E. promotes "the release of the dynamic emotions of pain, fear, anger and hurt which are then replaced with love, acceptance and support". In the R.O.A.R.E. encounter there is only one restrictive rule: no physical violence is allowed. The participants are encouraged to progress as rapidly as possible through what is called the thinking level (described as being superficial and ineffective) to the control level, "when the emotions begin to come out, the voice lowers, stuttering occurs, eyes close, subjects begin to shift in their seats and muscles start to spasm". Finally the body level is reached. This is described as the "gut level, the only real process. Control is released . . . intellect is inactive and there is complete trust in the therapists around you." This exhilarating process is then said to carry the subject to a stage of "euphoria, light-headedness and total lack of inhibition". In the course of one of these encounters the subjects commonly reach that point of disinhibition in which they crawl about on the floor, grasp one another desperately, weep, and literally roar.

The resocialization of the adult is progressively more certain the more closely his ultimate condition can be caused to approach that of infantile helplessness and dependence on the supportive influence of the milieu. An example of the intentional promotion of regression is that of anaclitic therapy. In this approach a central and guiding belief is that the subject has been fixed rigidly in the trap of his adult mind, that this entangling net must be rent, and that he must be caused to regress to some pre-logical level of psychosexual development. From this toti-potential condition his personality must then be resynthesized in the image of the omniscient therapist. In short, he is caused to be reborn.

It follows then that as long as the subject remains a mature adult, in complete control of his intellect and in close touch with the environment that he has learned to adapt to with the least amount of psychic stress, he will remain resistant to the techniques of resocialization. Proponents of behaviour control are therefore especially concerned to satisfy, as completely as it is possible to do, and in a variety of limiting circumstances, at least five basic requirements. The effectiveness of the resocializing process will vary according to the degree to which these principles can be applied but we must recognize that even in circumstances in which the controllers are most limited the impact of the techniques available to them may be considerable.

The subject must be isolated from his accustomed environment. The prison setting at Rahway and the remoteness of Esalen at Big Sur are examples of this. The subject must be protected from the countervailing influences of his family, work place and community. Moreover the resocializing institutions must maintain continuous surveillance over the subject. He must be totally dependent on the institution for all of his physical needs. This is why growth centres are ideally established in isolated places where the feeling of remoteness is intense and the usual flow of consensually validating stimuli is stopped.

The second requirement is that *there must be a complete suppression of past statuses.* When the subject enters the growth centre he is immediately stripped of his former status. In this way his concept of his former role is ignored and finally rejected. Status in the institution must be gained only through conformity to the values and behaviour approved by the group, and therefore indirectly by the controllers.

The third requirement is that *there must be a denial of the moral worth of the old self.* Thus the subject becomes a penitent, and as such encouraged to regard his past performances and beliefs as faulty. A radically new system of values is presented to him and in the course of time, he should ideally come to recognize that this new view of reality is decidedly superior to the one he previously subscribed to.

The fourth requirement is that *the subject must participate actively* in his own resocialization. Accordingly he must come to understand that it is essential for him to engage in self-analysis and self-criticism. In effect he must confess—and this with the utmost sincerity—to the defects of his personality and the errors he has committed over a very long period of time.

The fifth requirement is that *the resocializing institution must present negative sanctions.* Obviously if the subject is a prisoner he may be threatened with a variety of deprivations and tortures. However it is now well known that the threat of social disapproval and ostracism is exceedingly potent. The controllers who are currently denied the more extreme forms of negative sanction have, nevertheless, a powerful instrument in the form of peer-group pressure. And, of course, positive sanctions may be equally guiding. The evangelist offers the reward of salvation. The Chinese Communists offer the satisfaction of right-thinking citizenship. The centres for human potential offer enhanced creativity. The management development controller offers the reward of enlightened leadership and increased productivity.

Perhaps it is only fortuitous that a very unsettling word is used in the following statement but it may be worth referring to a naive comment by a lower-level supervisor in an attempt to describe his experience in Phase I of an organization development programme: "Well there are two ways you can change. One is that you can do it by attrition but this takes too long. The other is that you can do it like the Chinese do it—by brainwashing. Now this may sound critical and I don't mean it that way, but this is how the Grid Training Programme was done. You were under conditions of pressure and you kept getting these theories repeated to you over and over, and it has worked."

Now there is no reason for us to suppose that this man had any real comprehension of the techniques of brainwashing. It must be said, however, that repetition, the application of massive social pressure, a sense of urgency, a feeling of great purpose, and the insistence that the veracity of the leaders must be unquestioned are all characteristics held in common by the directors of managerial grid training, the revival meeting, such quasi-religious systems as Scientology, and political brainwashing. These techniques do work and all of them are based on the assumption that the individual must relinquish his identity and immerse himself in the group in the interests of some greater good.

No one who has lived all his life in mainland China has ever lived under a regime that was other than totalitarian. In pre-revolutionary China the dreaded Kuomintang maintained an institution known as Pao Chia in which ten households were formed into groups and ten groups into still larger masses all for the purpose of checking the intrusion of communistic thought and subversive activity in general. During the savage Japanese regime people in most of the great cities of China were utterly lacking in freedom. Since the triumph of the Communists in 1949, an astounding transformation has taken place in China but the price the people have paid for their real progress has been subjection to a degree of conformity and group control that is absolutely appalling. In the matter of behaviour control, and thought control too, the Chinese are far in advance of the Russians, who now seem highly stratified and even bourgeois by comparison.

Many of the techniques used in China are based on the work of the great Russian neurophysiologist I. P. Pavlov. In effect the citizen must be conditioned to accept uncritically and even joyously the ideas offered by the regime as representing the ultimate in social truth and virtue. Three related aspects of the Chinese approach to resocialization may be considered: the treatment of the individual reactionary, the mass indoctrination used before 1966, and the function of the cadre schools established during the Cultural Revolution.

The Chinese Communist prison regulations state: "In dealing with the criminals, there shall be regularly adopted measures of corrective study classes, individual interviews, study of assigned documents, and organized discussions to educate them in the admission of guilt and obedience to the law, political and current events, labour production and culture, so as to expose the nature of the crime committed, thoroughly wipe out criminal thoughts, and establish a new moral code."

The experience of Dr. Vincent, a Westerner who had practiced medicine for many years in Shanghai, is particularly illustrative. Vincent was suddenly arrested and taken to a re-education centre where he spent the next three and a half years. He was incarcerated in a room eight feet by 12 along with eight Chinese prisoners who were well advanced in their rehabilitation and accordingly eager to assist in the reformation of the new criminal. Addressed only by his prison number, Vincent was made to sit in the centre of this group and respond to their denunciations to the effect that he was an imperialist spy and an enemy of the People's Republic. From the beginning, then, the prisoner must give up his identity. Vincent was no longer a doctor: he was a nameless spy cleverly masquerading as a doctor.

These group sessions alternated with extended periods in which Vincent would be interrogated by a judge. He was kept constantly awake, fed minimally and subjected to continuous anxiety. Because he first denied his guilt the judge ordered that his hands be chained behind his back. Later his feet were also chained; and in this condition he would again have to endure the marathon encounters with his cellmates. Vincent had to eat his thin broth from a bowl on the floor in the manner of a dog.

The next phase of the process was the promotion of self-betrayal. Vincent was made to denounce his friends and relatives and in so doing reduce his own self-respect to nil. This reinforced his sense of utter isolation and dependence on his captors. He entered the phase of total conflict in which he was no longer certain what was true and what was false. He saw that he was about to be annihilated totally as a human being. At this point, and imagining that he might be shot at any moment, Vincent gave up any pretence at resistance. This was the eighth day of his captivity. A confession began to pour from him which over the next two months was constantly improved and embellished. Vincent was afflicted with a compulsion to confess and this state was responded to by signs of leniency on the part of the judge. The prisoner expressed his profound gratitude to the judge and also towards his cellmates for having assisted him to recognize at last the true nature and extent of his criminal activity.

Three weeks after the lenient phase began Vincent started a group re-education programme which occupied up to sixteen hours daily. A leader would read from a piece of Communist literature and each member of the group was expected to comment on this and criticize the statements made by the others. These discussions were in fact totally lacking in intellectual content. The prisoners engaged in the analysis of feelings and beliefs. Failure to participate with enthusiasm would result in demotion to an earlier phase of the programme, and even the re-application of the chains. The prisoners were now referred to as school-mates and the officials were instructors.

During the following year Vincent revised his official confession several times on the basis of what he had learned about himself from his schoolmates. In the end he had learned to criticize every detail of his behaviour strictly in terms of Maoist doctrine. He had reached the phase of progress and harmony and was able to produce a final, entirely perfect, confession.

After the Communist takeover in 1949, every effort was made by the regime to induce guilt in those who retained some attachment to the capitalist system. According to Sargant: "Orgies of group confession about political deviation were encouraged. The denouncing of parents and relatives by their children—as under Hitler—added to the desired atmosphere of insecurity and anxiety." This was accompanied by a reign of terror remarkably similar to the ones in 18th-century France under Robespierre, and later in Russia under Stalin. There were mass trials in sports arenas, where reactionaries were publicly humiliated and publicly shot. The Communist officials called this "the campaign for the suppression of counter-revolutionaries with fanfare".

Apart from these great spectacles the Chinese also made extensive use of small-group training, which makes the Chinese experience particularly relevant to the subject of this book. These training courses all took place at isolated camps. Students were kept in a condition of constant mental and physical fatigue. Tension was always maintained at a high level. At these camps the trainees knew they had to learn, because resistant students were continually disappearing from the scene.

The trainees were divided into small groups of about ten, and in these groups the language was vicious and humour was utterly lacking. In each group an informer was always present but this man was so well disguised that he could never be certainly identified. One characteristic of the Chinese ideological group that is still not used in American organizational development groups was the writing of autobiographical statements. These comprehensive narratives were read and criticized in the small groups. They would then be revised to reflect an even more perfect understanding of Maoist thought and would finally become the property of the state.

Walker points out that within six months of training the crisis occurs. This state tended to develop in most of the members of the group at about the same time and was characterized by hysterical weeping. The trainers made use of the suggestibility that is a basic aspect of this contagious breakdown to bring about final conversion to the ideas of the revolutionary culture. After four more months of reinforcement the students were released to proselytize on behalf of the revolution in every part of China.

Today the Chinese do not tend to refer to the years before 1949: they refer to the years before 1966 during which, in spite of great effort, revisionist tendencies began to threaten the purity of the revolution. It was in 1966 that Chairman Mao launched his Cultural Revolution and for the following three years intensive Maoist activity brought about the reindoctrination of most of the population. Since that time there has been not the slightest tolerance of freedom or individuality in any sense that would be meaningful to a citizen of a liberal democratic state.

This Great Proletarian Cultural Revolution was actually carried out in four phases. The first, beginning quietly in 1964, involved the creation of public opinion. The second, in 1966, was the exposure and criticism of the people whom the party called "Capitalist Roaders". The Red Guards dressed many of these people in dunce's caps, drove them around on the tops of trucks so that the crowds might jeer at them, and forced them to humiliate themselves at savage public rallies.

The third phase was the seizure of power and the formation of revolutionary committees (1968). The fourth phase is still going on. It is the period of "struggle, criticism, and transformation". Mao had determined that the old class structure was beginning to re-emerge. Elitism was being revived. The Chairman, accordingly, called forth his militant Red Guards and exhorted them to carry the Cultural Revolution to the people. Everywhere three-in-one alliances were formed of revolutionary party cadres, People's Liberation Army representatives, and revolutionary masses. These committees now operate by means of open discussion, unremitting public criticism and concensus agreement. Every issue and every decision is political. Every aspect of the life of a Chinese citizen is controlled by the Maoist ideology and the real enemy is always the terrible possibility of his entertaining a revisionist thought.

In order to protect the people from such crime the May 7 cadre schools were created. Built in rural wasteland, these schools are designed to reacquaint the urban cadre with the simple, self-reliant peasant virtues. The cadres, hundreds at a time, are sent to these places to build dormitories, factories, farms and classrooms. They remain there at least six months, but sometimes far longer if their political sickness is severe. The real purpose of the cadre school is to resocialize the people. There is nothing voluntary about attendance and it is the intention of Peking to send not only the potentially dangerous government workers, school teachers and other professionals to these schools, but everyone.

Here the cadres re-examine themselves. They spend about half of their time doing hard physical labour; but otherwise they study the writings of Chairman Mao, the Marxist classics, the history of the French Revolution and, of course, Lenin on "State and Revolution". They also attend group meetings where they confess to their political errors and where others probe for their ideological weaknesses. A basic dictum of the Cultural Revolution was to "rely on the masses". The cadre, therefore, has to personally experience the life-style of the peasant and factory worker. He has to give up his status, mingle with the people, listen to them as they describe the horrors of life under the old regime, identify with them, and become one of them. He is to accomplish this by surrendering his privacy and by offering himself whole-heartedly to the group. The purpose of the cadre group is to raise the consciousness of class struggle and to combat revisionist patterns of thought. This goal is not even slightly concealed. The administrator or office worker or doctor is told that he must be reoriented by the peasants. He must work, live, eat and study with them so that these folk will purge him of his bourgeois tendencies. At the school the peasants and the other cadres criticize him until he confesses and begs for forgiveness. This is held to be the only method of returning to ideological health. In the group meetings men and women of all ages publicly condemn themselves while a secretary records every word. They issue their confessions with much colour and emotion; they denounce their evil associates and relatives; and they indicate that they have regained their unswerving loyalty to Chairman Mao, and their absolute dedication to the goals of the Cultural Revolution. Under the peculiar circumstances that obtain today in China it would be unthinkable for anyone to deviate in the slightest from the norms of the group and, by extension, of the state. The cadre schools are, of course, described as educative, not punitive; but it is well understood that ideological impurity is a crime and re-education at the school may, in difficult cases, take a very long time.

There is absolutely no doubt that the Chinese have put into practice a system of resocialization that satisfies every one of the requirements noted at the beginning of this chapter. And they have accomplished this in a population of eight hundred million people.

In certain interesting respects, the cadre schools of China resemble the human growth centres that have appeared on this continent in the last few years. Yet there are a number of very important differences. In matters relating to ideology there is no surrounding spirit of free inquiry in China. No one can question the ideas of the system when to do so is regarded as evidence of sickness, the treatment of which consists in an even more intensive programme of re-education. In our own resocialization centres the participants are encouraged to criticize and confess but they are also exhorted to attack the great institutions of society, such as the legal, educational, political, economic and marital systems on the grounds that these must all be radically changed. There is nothing anarchistic about the May 7 cadre schools. China is a depressed and incredibly puritan country and all overt manifestations of physical contact between people is abhorred. In our own growth centres such physical contact is often encouraged as a specific and necessary antidote to what is regarded as a cruelly repressive culture. In China everything is done collectively and everyone is at all times under surveillance. This is precisely the situation that obtains in our human growth centres but from these centres people return to the free and private environments of their homes. The Chinese leave the cadre schools to return to neighbourhoods, factories and offices that are organized to reinforce the political consciousness of the citizens. Innovation of the sort so extravagantly admired in our own growth centres would be unthinkable in China. And that is because in China the people's utopia is held to be perfect and, as such, beyond reproach. It is the people who must be modified to fit the system, and not the other way around.

We will discover, however, that although such personal growth centres as Esalen could not possibly be tolerated in China, our many organizational development centres would be recognized and appreciated there. The Chinese would say, however, that in these O.D. centres ideological reorientation would be more certain if the risks could be considerably increased. I have heard proponents of organizational development say precisely this to me on this continent; and, of course, they are absolutely right. I recall being told by an enthusiastic T-group trainer that to understand the nature of anything one must experience that thing at first hand. He said, for example, that one could know nothing about the Philippines unless one had lived in that country for many years. You had to become part of the life of the Philippines and participate in the process of changing the very nature of that society. He said: "If you want to know the taste of a pear, you must change the pear by eating it yourself."

Chairman Mao Tse-Tung wrote in 1937: "Whoever wants to

know a thing has no way of doing so except by coming into contact with it, that is, by living in its environment. If you want to learn the taste of a pear, you must change the pear by eating it yourself . . . if you want to know the theory and methods of revolution you must take part in revolution. All genuine knowledge originates in direct experience."

4

The Human Potential Movement

Sigmund Freud was undoubtedly one of the most creative men of our time. When he died in London in 1939, at the age of 83, no one took his place. Certainly Jacob Moreno did not take his place, even though according to many people this is in fact what happened.

In the early years of this century Freud had a number of disciples to whom he played the role of jealous father and chief creator. One after another, nearly all these men broke away from the great father. Usually, they isolated certain details of Freud's thinking and developed these bits into immense theories by which all could be explained. It was thus, with much ill feeling, that C. G. Jung departed from the flock to develop his mystical views of the persona and the collective unconscious. And Otto Rank ran off to believe that all anxiety could be referred to the trauma of birth. And Adler. And Ferenczi. And many others including, interestingly, Freud himself, when in the early 'twenties he repudiated many of his earlier ideas and went off in another direction. A number of his supporters found such things as the new death instinct quite unpleasant: they remained behind as orthodox 1906 Freudians and this school has persisted, virtually unchanged, to the present day.

For very different reasons, Moreno was among the unimpressed. It did not matter to him what Freud did next because quite obviously Freud had an *idée fixe* regarding the individual and his instinctual drives. The terms might change but the determinism always remained. Actually quite a number of others were troubled by Freud's failure to agree that society was every bit as important in forming one's personality as his sexual and aggressive urges. Karen Horney was certainly one of these and so, most significantly, was the great American Harry Stack Sullivan. For Moreno, however, none of these people went nearly far enough in the direction of the here and now, of acting out, of involvement with people in the present.

In orthodox psychoanalysis the patient reclines on a couch and free-associates. He says everything that comes into his head and the analyst rarely speaks at all. But what if the patient wants to dance? What if he wants to pray, shout at his wife, roll on the floor, pretend he is six years old? He just cannot do these things in this formal setting. He must not act out his impulses; he must restrain them and just talk.

In 1921 Moreno founded the Stegreiftheater—the "theatre of spontaneity"—in the Maysedergasse near the Vienna Opera. It was here that he turned Aristotle inside out and managed in the process to develop a most remarkable therapeutic instrument. In his *Poetics* Aristotle observed that Greek drama tended to purify the spectators by causing them to experience certain emotions. Through high art there was catharsis, emotional relief, but this great benefit was felt only by the audience. Of course Aristotle was quite right, and it remains true today that it is the audience that experiences the anger, sexual arousal, depression, sympathy, anxiety or intellectual awareness. The players reproducing the work for the tenth time are not purified by the work of the author. Indeed the more thoroughly skilled the artists are, the less vulnerable they will be to accidents of emotion in the course of performance.

Yet in Vienna Moreno discovered elements in his theatre of spontaneity that caused emotional release not only in the audience but also in the cast. His actors, he discovered, were learning something about themselves; they were developing insight into the patterns of their interpersonal behaviour and this insight was both exciting and useful. Moreno refined the procedure and at some point in the process created Psychodrama. Paul Stefan of Vienna's *Die Stunde* wrote on May 5, 1924: "Vienna has an ensemble under the direction of J. L. Moreno which, instead of reproducing written lines, improvises them on the spot. I assure you that this can be more amusing and impressive than the work of all our classicists, including Strindberg".

By the time Moreno moved to New York in 1925 the essential technique of Psychodrama had emerged. Now it must be clearly understood that in Psychodrama neither director nor players try to create art. It was my impression when I visited the Moreno Institute in New York a few years ago that art was an occasional result, certainly, but never the primary goal.

There was no script and no case history. There were simply people on a small circular stage saying things to one another with incredible spontaneity. A production was fragmentary, checked with flashbacks, broken with changes of scene, disrupted by the introduction of new characters drawn from the surrounding audience, halted by silence, tripped up by irrelevance; and confused by role reversals and various other curious techniques peculiar to the form. The production happened in the present though it sometimes described things that would happen in the future, or had happened in the past. If that scene were set in Miami in 1941 then it was happening right at that moment as it did then, and the protagonist was several decades younger. That is to say if the subject was thirty and he referred to an event that had happened when he was six then he was six. He was six and he was on the beach at Miami throwing a beach ball to his father. Another player—an auxiliary ego—played the part of the father, and the imaginary ball was tossed back and forth. A few minutes later the scene might be in Columbus and the protagonist would be in a kitchen talking to a woman playing the part of his wife. In a moment it was many years later, and he was dead, talking to God. Free association was replaced by free acting out. The formal design of the psychiatrist's office was replaced by a three-dimensional social space.

This space need not have been a proper theatre. There is no doubt that the theatre added to the excitement of the production. In Beacon, New York, a few miles north of the city, Moreno built his Theatre of Psychodrama. It was a very remarkable structure. The main stage was a circular platform about fifteen feet in diameter. One step lower than this stage there was another circular platform about four feet wide, and a step below this yet another platform about six feet wide. A step below this was the floor of the theatre. Only the top circle was complete. The middle platform was interrupted by pillars upstage and the lower platform cut off by stairways on each side that ascended to a balcony overlooking centre stage. Spectators faced nearly three sides of the stage, and in fact people could sit on the lower platform to surround the highest stage entirely.

On this structure a human conflict was located and explored. The whole production was guided by Moreno. Someone would volunteer to be the protagonist and leave the audience group to join the director on the stage. Props were extremely minimal, consisting of perhaps a couple of chairs and a table on the central stage. (In the past, experiments had been tried in which someone who could draw very rapidly had dashed off an appropriate backdrop for each new scene. This device seemed unnecessary and by this time Moreno was no longer using it.)

A conversation began that was quite similar to the beginning of any psychiatric interview. After a few minutes the patient disclosed that in the morning he had been a little irritated with his wife. The whole scene suddenly became three-dimensional.

Moreno was on his feet. He drew another patient from the audience and told her she was the patient's wife. The scene was set in the patient's dining-room. The time was that very morning. The two patients sat a little self-consciously and said nothing to one another. Moreno walked to the first patient and stood behind his chair. He said to the woman: "What are you so fed up about this morning"? She was a bit startled but blurted out: "It's not me. It's you." The patient then said: "It is, eh?" This time he spoke with some conviction. Moreno stepped out of the picture.

Woman: "That's right. You can hardly wait to get out of here."

Patient: "No. She wouldn't have said that. My wife wouldn't have said that."

Moreno: "All right." (*To the patient*) "You. You be your own wife." (*To the woman*) "You be him." This technique, called "role reversal", is typified by Moreno as: "And when you are near I will tear your eyes out and place them instead of mine, and you will tear my eyes out and will place them instead of yours. Then I will look at you with your eyes and you will look at me with mine."

Moreno: "Start the scene again."

Woman (as patient): "What are you so fed up about this morning?"

Patient (as his wife): "You're the one that's fed up."

Woman (as patient): "Is that so?"

Patient (as his wife): "That's right. What do you care about what day of the month it is for me?"

Moreno: "All right. You are yourself now. Go on."

Patient (as himself): "Sure, I care. Look, I do care. I know what you go through."

Woman (as wife): "You're not considerate of me in lots of ways."

Patient: "Well, how do you think I feel? How about last month? Jersey City."

Moreno: "You're in Jersey City. Begin this scene."

The dialogue was banal. It was not meant to be artistic. The idea was merely to give this man an opportunity to express his feelings as vividly as possible and it was intended that in the course of all this he would learn something about his own interpersonal relationships.

The auxiliary egos (the woman patient in the example above) might be patients or specially trained assistants. The production was extremely flexible. If the patient mentioned a dream and the director felt it should be illustrated then this is precisely what was done. If in this dream there was a chorus of people singing, then the audience was caused to sing. The lights were dimmed and brightened. Action took place in the balcony, in the audience, and on all three levels. There were soliloquies, mirror techniques, role reversals, rapid changes from the past to the future, and from Iceland to Brooklyn.

After seeing *After the Fall,* Moreno wrote a dialogue between Thespis and himself.

Thespis: "I just came from seeing Miller's play *After the Fall.*"

Moreno: "What did you find?"

Thespis: "It's a psychodrama. What a calamity for the theatre of Aeschylus and Sophocles, even for the theatre of Shakespeare! I feel miserable but you should be proud of it."

The argument proceeded for some time and every technique of psychodrama was discovered in the play. Finally, however, Moreno denied that *After the Fall* was a psychodrama. It was only the conserve of the psychodrama, he said. Once it had been written down and tape-recorded it was no longer spontaneous. By definition it was not a psychodrama, because it was frozen.

In time, as we shall see, Moreno's quite brilliant invention was debased by the entrepreneurs of the human potential movement. It became only another flashy trick in the bursting carpet bags of the radical humanists.

It is quite impossible to identify, with any certainty, all of the sources of today's Human Potential Movement. We know, of course, that there have been numerous utopian societies in the past and that many of these produced literatures which, after varying periods of time, were rediscovered and referred to by people with similar aims and urges. Such influences were discontinuous and therefore quite haphazard. Other influences can be shown to be continuous with certain social phenomena of our time and it seems to me that they are of very particular interest.

Of these I am inclined to think that the social experiments in Palestine, particularly in the 'twenties, are of the greatest significance. The men who conceived of the idea of Israel were themselves greatly influenced by the awakening of national consciousness throughout Eastern Europe in the 19th Century. During this period many of the more active members of the oppressed Jewish community joined socialistically-oriented Zionist organizations, and dreamed about emigration to Palestine.

A new myth was created. A modern Eden was to be brought into being and this utterly free and just society would be the most ideal utopia ever to appear on Earth. The early pioneers were immensely affected by this mystical conception of the creation of a new society and a correspondingly new man. At this time Russian radicalism had an enormous influence on the new colonies. Some of the early pioneers denounced private ownership of land as the greatest evil of civilization. Others, under the particular influence of Aaron David Gordon, worshipped labour. Gordon held that it was only through hard physical labour that a man could be redeemed. *"Frailich! . . . Frailich! . . . Frailich! . . ."* ("Joy! . . . Joy! . . . Joy! . . . ") was a condition that could be achieved only by slaving endlessly in the sacred fields of Palestine.

These and no doubt many other influences led inexorably toward the invention of the kibbutz, and this remarkable institution seems to be a most significant antecedent of the human potential movement of today. It was in 1907 that a group of restless immigrants who had escaped from the poverty and persecution of eastern Europe declared a strike against the overseer of a farm. Arthur Ruppin, director of the Zionist Settlement Office in Jaffa, sided with the strikers, fired the overseer and agreed to let the workers run the farm on a communal basis. There had been many perfect communities of this sort in the past, of course. The Essenes were probably an example of this. The Doukhobors of Russia and the early Mormons of the United States were others. All these people voluntarily opted out of the prevailing society to create an ideal society of their own. In such places only the most zealous devotees to the cause were able to survive. The citizens of every new Jerusalem desire to be utterly free and equal, and invariably, every man is to have an equal share in government. As always, of course, this extreme libertarian tendency produced in the course of time a tyranny of its own. The majority were so certain of their rectitude that any divergent minority was considered utterly intolerable. In this connection Amos Elon observed: "There is little that can be as demanding and restricting to an individual's liberty as service to an extreme form of libertarianism."

One of the most important of these very radical *kibbutzim* was a brotherhood called Bittania that appeared in the early 'twenties. The communards of Bittania especially hated bourgeois values and everything that was tainted with conformity. Their leader was an exceptionally charismatic man named Meir Yaari and under his direction the men and women of Bittania laboured in the fields up to fourteen hours a day. The real life of Bittania, however, took place in the evening when the members engaged in the *sicha* or conversation. In the sicha members revealed their most private secrets. They spoke of their sexual anxieties, outlined their fantasies, and disclosed all their doubts and personal grievances.

It was perfectly acceptable at Bittania for people to engage in sexual intercourse with any other member of the commune. It was, however, an unspeakable act of selfishness if these lovers failed subsequently to share their most intimate feelings on the affair with the assembled commune. Fifty years later, a nearly identical rule was honoured in many of the encounter sessions held at the Esalen Institute in California. The communards made a similar fetish of openness and honesty, but we must remember that in addition they toiled in the fields for ten to fourteen hours a day, seven days a week. At Esalen there seems to be no such recognition of the virtue of hard physical labour.

Another fascinating source is the work of the American Frank Buchman. In the 'twenties this passionate believer in moral rectitude discovered that confession must precede conversion. Buchman accordingly invented what he called "conscience therapy". In this technique the subject was encouraged to review his frailties in the presence of other people. Buchman held that any man could be changed, that a man so changed could change others, and that if enough men were changed the world would be saved. At the time he founded the Student Christian Movement he believed most fervently in the principle that self-discovery could be achieved through self-examination within a group. He called this "coming clean". Later he founded the Oxford Group, an organization that especially developed the house-party technique. The similarity between this technique and that used by the encounter group is very striking indeed. Later Buchman went on to found Moral Re-Armament and the movement became very powerful in the years before the Second World War.

Buchman was persuaded that the "Five Cs" were an excellent guide to the good life: confidence, confession, conviction, conversion and continence. It is only the last of these alliterative aids that has failed to survive into the modern group movement.

It is apparent then that the movement did not spring fully armed from the wise head of any single thinker. We must observe, however, that the forerunners of the movement invariably tended to be deadly serious. Wesley's Classes and Mao's cadre groups were not noted for their light-heartedness. All these sources have tended to be fixed in the service of some ideological or religious cause: and people advancing ideal solutions to the world's problems have never been particularly receptive to either skepticism or laughter.

So it has been with the modern history of the movement. There are many intriguing similarities between an 18th-century Wesleyan Class and a modern American class of high-school freshmen earnestly engaged in a sensitivity session. Both classes may be seen as being exquisitely vulgar and anti-intellectual; both emphasize raw feeling rather than rationality; both are established so that the participants will be enriched either in the hereafter or in the here and now. In the first case the believers come to experience the joy of salvation; in the second the reward is the joy of disinhibition. In both the leaders would be quick to rise to any suspected affront. What they are doing is self-evidently good, and anyone who does not see that this is so is clearly in need of the very service being criticized.

There are also many differences, of course, and this analogy can most certainly not be carried too far. For one thing the Methodist effect on England was basically a cohesive one. In this respect the Great Revival was similar to most religious movements in that it tended to cause people to accept their lot and invest most of their energy in the more desperate matter of their salvation. The sensitivity class in Westchester County is the product of a movement that has had a far more pervasive influence on the society. That is to say some of the elements of the movement have tended to weaken the society and others have tended to strengthen it. As time has gone on the deracinating elements have come to dominate the movement but at the beginning of its modern history the emphasis was relentlessly altruistic.

The modern period may arbitrarily be said to begin with the emigration to the United States of the psychologist Kurt Lewin. This wise and intensely humane man escaped from Nazi Germany in 1933, and it was his constant concern to discover how the slashing bigotry of totalitarianism might be prevented. His early work in group dynamics became the basis of much that was to follow, including both the benefits and the wild excesses. If he could survey the small group field today, Lewin would certainly be appalled, but in the 'thirties it seemed to him that the group might be used to enormous advantage in reducing the tension and misunderstanding that seemed almost as rife in the U.S. as in Germany. His concept of force-field analysis anticipated a tendency that was to become one of the most unfortunate characteristics of the modern movement. He held that immediate forces are far more important than distant ones and in this he was hardly wrong. In simpler minds, the concept led to the belief that the past and the far removed were not just less important than the present time and the living space, but utterly lacking in significance of any kind.

Lewin was one of the founders of the Research Center for Group Dynamics at M.I.T. and also of the Commission on Community Relations of the American Jewish Congress. These involvements led him to organize a Basic Skills Training Group for the Connecticut Interracial Commission, an event that must in retrospect be seen as one of the great landmarks in the history of the movement. In Connecticut, Lewin stated that you could tell people what to do for a long time but that this would never be as useful as letting people discover these things for themselves. Experience, then, became a second fundamental characteristic of the movement, and excesses traceable to this essentially useful truism became, in time, outrageous and inane. Lewin also said: "It is usually easier to change individuals formed into a group than to change any one of them separately." In 1946, the Connecticut Commission began to bring black and white people together to discuss the question of racial tension. After each day's session, Lewin and his staff met to hear reports from four observers of the work groups. These observers reported on such matters as decision making, group climate, interaction and leadership. The commission members found this novel feedback from observers both refreshing and useful. In fact this part of the day was more interesting than the conference itself. The observers were then asked to participate in the meetings so that they might react immediately whenever they saw something that seemed to be relevant to the group process. Such terms as "participant-observer" and "feedback" which eventually became fearful cliches in the movement were altogether new in 1946, and generated much excitement.

In 1947 Leland Bradford, Kenneth Benne, and Ronald Lippitt founded the National Training Laboratory at Bethel, Maine. This new organization was originally a division of the National Education Association. The founders were convinced that groups could be used to re-educate people in such a way as to change their values, behaviours and attitudes. All three men were much influenced by Lewin, and the principles of experiential learning and feedback were used from the beginning at the Gould Academy in Bethel. Shortly thereafter groups that discussed their own processes were called T-groups at Bethel. The "T" stood for training, and the impulse toward reorientation implied in this word became an essential characteristic of the Human Potential Movement that clearly emerged from this early work at Bethel.

The original T-group is at first sight a very simple thing. About twelve people gather in a room with a leader or trainer. The trainer may indicate how much time is available for the session, and he may also explain briefly that the purpose of the affair is to allow people to achieve a fuller understanding of their own and other people's behaviour. And that is all. The group is entirely lacking in structure, there is no stated goal, no task of any kind, and no leadership. The people usually sit in an irregular circle and anyone is allowed to say anything that occurs to him. There is usually an extended awkwardness during which hesitant observations and silences serve to confuse the participants and arouse their hostility towards the leader, who has abdicated his traditional responsibility to lead.

By now, of course, nearly everyone knows the rules of this

game very well. Very few people come to a T-group these days without some understanding of the fact that the focus is to be on the here and now and that flights of memory, or excursions into future plans, will not be honoured. Specialized learning is a thing of no value in the T-group. Social position or authority are similarly of no interest. The participants are all equal and they are expected to interact just as they are, and where they are. The emphasis is on the feelingful or affective: the cognitive aspects of the mind are not of any particular interest except in so far as such intellectual activity is considered as standing in the way of authenticity.

Feedback, according to Lewin's discovery of this process, is essential. Participants thus reveal their several responses to the things that other people have said, with the emphasis always on how they feel about these things. In this way the members are said to "learn" how other people feel about their behaviour, their personality, their attitudes and sentiments. Feedback engenders, of course, more of the same, and before long a complex melange of feelings is roiling about the room, and everyone is presumably benefitting from this laboratory education. A common expression among devotees of this variety of education is, "What is happening between X and Y?" or simply: "What is happening?"

Anxiety is characteristic of the T-group seminars and for a very simple reason. In the course of his life every person has learned an elaborate system of mental defences which, in most situations, serves him well. In the peculiar circumstance of the T-group these defences, in so far as they are detected by the other members, become a primary conversational topic. In the T-group he who maintains his ordinary modes of behaviour is sooner or later centred by the group and specifically subjected to close examination. If he defends himself he discovers that this results only in a more intense assault. There is no defence, particularly no intellectual defence, against those who would have you step forth naked and unsophisticated into a group of strangers. Because a person's usual way of interacting with others is completely blocked, anxiety is the certain result. This state of anxiety is considered essential to the learning process, however. Without it, change in the direction of the new culture of the group would not occur, and the group purpose would be thwarted.

The T-group is a microcosm of the sort of society proposed by the magic humanists. It is egalitarian and utterly permissive. In the T-group, every feeling may be expressed, and the response of the other members will be vigorously non-evaluative. At least this is what is claimed by proponents of the form. It is true that it is not acceptable to raise eyebrows concerning any particular revelation because everyone is carefully tolerant and accepting. Eyebrows are raised nevertheless, because there is one crime that can never be forgiven in the T-group, and that crime is failure to participate in what is held to be an open and honest way. A woman might reveal her most intimate secret that she entertains from time to time the serious desire to strangle her infant children: everyone will be aggressively understanding and supportive. If, on the other hand, this same woman responds with a cool smile when another member accuses her of harbouring hostility towards him she will be savagely attacked for her heartless denial of authentic feedback.

The participant must give up role playing and just be himself, but if that self should be disinclined to reveal highly personal thoughts then that self will be condemned. Such a T-grouper will either have to submit to the interpersonal style of the others or become a very skilful actor in order to withhold his private thoughts and preserve an important aspect of his identity.

There is an underlying assumption in the group that the participant will learn how to expand his consciousness and become a more sensitive human being. In particular he will learn to see himself as others see him through constant feedback from the other participants. He will also become more adventurous concerning his way of living in the world and of living with other people. He will be less defensive and more willing to try new ways of dealing with the exigencies of life.

The T-group is always expected to re-educate the participants regarding the idea that the hierarchical form of society is passé. In the new and enlightened society people are interdependent and collaborative and the relationships are all non-linear. The authoritarian system is all finished now that it has been discovered that all men are absolutely equal by virtue of their common humanity. In the course of the T-group experience the vice-president will learn that he is no better able to exercise his midbrain than the office boy. If all men should be equal in the ideal society then all men will be made equal by the Procrustean bed of the group.

Procrustes was a very clever fellow. He lived beside the road to Athens and offered a night's lodging to tired travellers. Unfortunately he only had one bed, and this bed was of average size. If a short man should lie on it Procrustes racked him out to fit. In the case of a tall man the compulsive host sawed off as much of the sleeper's legs as projected beyond the end of the bed. Similarly if a person enters a group and displays there his learning and intelligence this deviance will be noted and condemned. It will be identified as a defence and ruthlessly lopped off. If a participant should have a very limited intelligence and no particular past experience he will be made to fit the group by being shown that such deficiencies count for nothing. If he can make use of his natural ability to be sensitive to the feelings of other people then he will be much appreciated. And everybody can do that. We all receive and understand simple verbal communications; we all pick up such non-verbal signs as inflection, facial expression and posture. In the group, however, everyone is expected to become even more tuned in to such things.

Several decades ago the American psychiatrist H. S. Sullivan talked about interpersonal relationships and particularly about empathy. Sullivan observed that the infant could detect the fine nuances of feeling emanating from its mother, and that it would respond to them. If the mother was minimally anxious, the infant would become restless and irritable. If the mother was contented the infant would become tranquil. Communications would flow between the members of this small emphatic system. In adults, this capacity to perceive non-verbal communication is not lost, but it tends to be obscured by the intrusion of complex language and, of course, cultural restraints. The sensitivity trainers are obsessed with this process of maturation because they think it blocks the only really meaningful sort of communication of which man is capable. This is why they are so delighted by juvenile or even infantile behaviour. The child, for them, is father to the man, but the man has been mentally crippled by both his intellect and his society. Fritz Perls, one of the great masters of the human potential movement, put this somewhat more vividly. He said we "mind-fuck" ourselves. It was Perls' mission in life to rehabilitate people who, through the use of their intelligence, learning and experience, tended to ravage their own minds.

"At the same time came the disciples unto Jesus, saying, Who is the greatest in the kingdom of heaven?

"And Jesus called a little child unto him, and set him in the midst of them.

"And said, Verily I say unto you, Except ye be converted, and become as little children, ye shall not enter into the kingdom of Heaven.

"Whosoever therefore shall humble himself as this little child, the same is greatest in the kingdom of heaven." (*Matthew 18:3*)

What we are confronted with is a revival of that utopian belief that the child at his simple play is innocent and beautiful. He is seen as marvellously forthright and hence authentic. He tends to keep all his emotions up front where they can be displayed at the drop of a stimulus. He weeps, shouts, throws things, turns somersaults of joy, without restraint or embarrassment. He has no burdensome task and his thoughtful penetration of the future is exceedingly limited. He is, it is repeatedly said, like the noble savage, another paradigm of guileless simplicity. The child would play as though he were living in the celestial garden, if

only the wicked society did not persistently intrude into his paradise with rules and exhortations and punishment. Nor is this
analogy in any sense foolish or lacking in significance. Later in
this book I will show that the tenets of the religion of human
potentialism have been especially applied in education, and the
result has been the widespread introduction of the open school
with its emphasis on the dictum, "Do what thou wilt." Children,
it is felt, should be protected against the rape of the mind so that
they will never lose their spontaneity and sense of joy.

The adults, participating in a T-group, must learn how to be
puerile again. They must discover that the smooth functioning
of the group is blocked by the intrusion of higher mental activity
and particularly of scepticism. And they must learn that group
interaction is facilitated by the eschewing of all defensive man-
oeuvres and the replacement with openness and honesty. Only
in this way can the seeker after more meaningful interpersonal
relationships learn the skills that his society failed to teach him.
Only in this way will he learn how to tune in all the time on his
own way of reacting to other people and to their way of reacting
to him.

Chris Argyris, one of the more rhapsodic exponents of the
T-group, has written: "Basically it is a group experience designed to provide maximum possible opportunities for the individuals to expose their behaviour, give and receive feedback,
experiment with new behaviour, and develop everlasting awareness and acceptance of self and others." It is the use of the word
"everlasting" that makes this statement particularly interesting.
A technique so potent that it will change people forever is
certainly one we ignore at great peril.

The assumption in the movement is that a person's cognitive
ability is not of any great importance. In the T-group he will
learn everything affectively. He will learn how to learn in this
way and then, at last, he will be a learned man. This may seem
preposterous to many people but in the Human Potential Movement it stands as a fundamental belief.

5

The Transparent Employee

From the beginning, the National Training Laboratory considered that its basic function was to help people relate better to one another in their places of work. Especially in the early years, the people who spent time at the laboratory at Bethel, Maine, were teachers, industrial managers, and men of the cloth. That the second group should have been so importantly represented might surprise some readers, but the fact is that for a number of years American business had been heavily bombarded with the charge that it was authoritarian and inhumane. The ideas of the anti-organization movement were increasingly fashionable during the late 'forties when the Industrial Relations Institute was created at the University of California. N.T.L. people were soon in contact with U.C.L.A., and the result was the founding of the Western Training Laboratories.

It was at this centre that the phrase "sensitivity training" was first used in 1954. A year earlier Kenneth Boulding published *The Organizational Revolution* in which he noted that love and justice were always overwhelmed by power and profit. In 1956, along came *The Organization Man* by William H. Whyte in which once again the individual humanity of the worker was seen as suppressed by the values and objectives of big business. In 1957, Chris Argyris pointed out that employee and manager had divergent goals: the worker wanted to realize his potential but the manager wanted to exploit that potential in the interests of greater productivity. Organizations were, he said, basically anti-humanistic.

Perhaps the most influential of the 'fifties critics of the large organization was Douglas McGregor, professor of industrial management at M.I.T. McGregor did not publish *The Human Side of Enterprise* until 1960, but many earlier papers and addresses preceded this definitive statement on "theory X" and "theory Y".

In conventional management—"theory X"—everything is done in the interest of economics. People are merely directed, motivated, controlled, and modified according to the needs of the organization. According to theory X this managerial intervention is required because without it the worker would be passive or even resistive with regard to the needs of the organization. Theory-X managers believe that their employees desire to work as little as possible and therefore must be led. Moreover, the worker is basically self-centred, hostile towards change, gullible, and not particularly bright. McGregor pointed out that this set of assumptions must be questioned.

Abraham Maslow of Brandeis University had held that man was a wanting animal. As soon as his needs on one level were taken care of he transferred all his attention to the satisfaction of needs on the next. Thus, a man deprived of oxygen is concerned entirely with this crucial lack. If he is allowed to breathe he becomes hungry. If he is fed, this need also ceases to be a motivator of his behaviour. When man's physiological needs are all taken care of he turns his attention to social needs and these begin to motivate his behaviour. He now desires associations, approval by his fellows, love, and a sense of belonging. He desires, in short, to join a group. But management, according to

McGregor, is hostile to this groupiness because it is afraid that the group may develop objectives inimical to those of the organization.

At an even higher level McGregor came upon the egoistic needs of man. These had to do with such things as self-esteem, and a desire to be independent, competent and learned. McGregor also noticed that people desired to be recognized and appreciated. At the highest level, McGregor discovered the need for self-fulfilment. Man needed to be creative. He needed, in fact, to realize his potentiality to the fullest possible extent.

At every level, theory-X management was a disastrous failure because it failed to appreciate the crucial importance of this hierarchical system of needs. It simply directed, manipulated and controlled, and therefore failed utterly. In response to this McGregor produced theory Y, and the walls of the pyramid were presumably expected to crumble before the astonished eyes of American management. According to theory Y, people are not passive, indolent and resistive to change. It is the task of management to provide the money, the material and the equipment, but after this is done it must create conditions under which the people can realize their own organizational objectives. Opportunities must be created so that growth may take place. In fact the potential of everyone must be unleashed. The guiding principle, then, was to be "management by objectives rather than management by control". McGregor said that people must be treated not as children but as mature adults.

How is this revolution in humanistic management to be brought about? McGregor talked a great deal about decentralization so that people would be free from the close control of the executive suite. They would be responsible for achieving their own objectives as independently as possible. He promoted what he called "participative and consultative management" and self-appraisal of performance on the part of the employee. McGregor announced: "The ingenuity and the perseverance of industrial management in the pursuit of economic gains have changed many scientific and technological dreams into commonplace realities. It is now becoming clear that the application of the same talent to the human side of enterprise will not only enhance substantially these materialistic achievements but will bring us one step closer to the 'good society'."

I do not doubt McGregor's essential altruism for one moment. It is appalling, however, to regard the progressive debasement of his ideas that began as far back as the late 'fifties. McGregor and others wanted to humanize the great corporation, an undoubtedly noble aim. The method that was soon used to bring all this about was the indiscriminate and involuntary use of the T-group, an instrument that, far from enhancing the depth and breadth of man, rendered him transparent for all to see. And then, with a further rationalizing twist, it was held that a man successfully reduced in this way must be more real, more authentic in every respect. There was then no more virtue in reticence or restraint. Understatement, honoured for some time as an indication of containedness, was deplored. Allusiveness, and the dignified withholding of certain intensely private thoughts and memories, were condemned. All was to be revealed and then, if this confession had been delivered convincingly enough in terms of the vulgar judgment of the group, one could expect to be a man whose potential had some chance of realization.

But I have not been discussing the furious excesses of the left wing of the encounter culture. I have been discussing the insinuation of the techniques of sensitivity training into corporations and branches of government. And this process has been very rapid and extraordinarily respectable. Organization Development or "orgment", as I am pleased to call it, has influenced a vast segment of the American business community in the last few years. Humble Oil, Ontario Hydro, Dow Chemical, the Aluminum Company of Canada, I.B.M., American Airlines, Procter and Gamble, General Electric, Union Carbide, and dozens of others, great and small, have invested much money, energy and, most importantly, human resources in it. On considering the great crisis in religion it is not surprising that the churches have grasped desperately for the alleged benefits of orgment. Methodists and Episcopalians have particularly been caught up in this new fad, and so has the American Red Cross. Universities across the continent have leapt eagerly on the sensitivity bandwagon, including Stanford, U.C.L.A., Brigham Young, Duke, Michigan State, Notre Dame, Wisconsin, the Harvard School of Business Administration, M.I.T.'s Sloane School of Industrial Management, the State University of New York at Buffalo, Syracuse, and dozens of others. Most commonly it has been the departments of psychiatry, psychology, social work and education that have been excited by the rage for sensitivity. In many cases participation in T-groups and encounters has been a course requirement, especially in departments that train mental-health workers. In terms of numbers of people involved sensitivity training has been a smashing success.

Orgment, of course, is clearly the right wing of the Human Potential Movement. Even so, deputies representing the views of the proponents of orgment would have sat far to the left of centre in the States General of France in 1789. In certain respects the insinuation of the principles of O.D. into an impressive array of large corporations and government departments on this continent is the most interesting manifestation of the Human Potential Movement.

It is one thing for the Y.M.C.A. to establish training laboratories for people who approach them voluntarily for this service. It is quite another thing for a government department of Social and Family Services to organize groups among its own personnel. This distinction is crucially important. In the case of the voluntary programmes co-ordinated by the independent growth centres the participant may, should he feel that the experience is not agreeable, terminate his association with the group at will. The worker in a private company or in one of the several government agencies that have introduced orgment is denied this freedom. His livelihood, he well knows, depends on his job, and it would not be comfortable for him to oppose for long the insistence on conformity to the Master Plan for Organizational Excellence.

Apart from the fact that it appears very modern, and therefore desirable, O.D. draws appeal by its promise to cause a quantum jump in terms of effectiveness in organizations that have begun to drift and stagnate. In such cases, it is held, nothing short of radical re-organization will revive the dying institution. Most significantly, the group must replace the individual. The human potential of all workers of the organization, from the chief executive to the cleaning lady, will be realized through participation in sensitivity training.

A consultant is retained. A plan, extending some years into the future, is drawn up. A top management group is designated. A strategic defence is arranged in anticipation of the emergence of people who might not only resist change but also be difficult to train. And then, little by little, the plan is implemented until all the workers are actively engaged in problem solving and communicating through the agency of the magical instrument known as the group.

We must consider the assumptions of Organization Development in much more detail. We must also examine the operational design of O.D., its significance to the individual, to the organization and to society, and its relation to the several other components of the Human Potential Movement. In undertaking this critical review of the nature and significance of the movement I am encouraged by a statement by Warren G. Bennis, one of the important contributors to the theory of Organization Development. In *The Managerial Revolution*, Bennis suggests: "Organizations should reward people who act as counter change agents to create forces against the seduction of novelty for its own sake." There is much more than foolish novelty that we must be concerned about, of course: but it is refreshing all the same to find even an inadequate note of caution in the Organization Development literature.

Now of course for a cultural idea to achieve such astonishing success, regardless of how dynamic and compelling it may be, there must first be created a social climate receptive to its introduction. The growth of the Human Potential Movement appears to be an indication that, rather suddenly, large numbers of people have concluded that to live in a complex and techno-logical society is to be deprived of joy. They have discovered that the movement offers to enrich their lives through the restoration of their capacity to feel and to be sensitive.

Of course it is true that at least some of the people who join these groups are motivated by mere curiosity, prurience or even a desire to experience a drug-free high, but it would be very unwise for us to fail to notice that there is, over all, a vast population of people who are now indicating a most urgent need for human contact. There is this need and it is very real indeed. The group has arisen to satisfy this need, and it is said to be extraordinarily successful in this regard.

We might conclude then that sensitivity training, since it is appreciated by so large a population, is successful because it works, and also that it is benign. Vast numbers of people would never approve of a cultural idea that would finally prove harm-ful. I would suggest at this point that we reject the notion of necessary correlation between benignity and popular success. In fact the history of civilization is strewn with the relics of magnificent social adventures extinguished by the even more persuasive ideas that very often lurked within them even as they flourished. Appreciation by the people has not always indicated that any new cultural element is valuable or even that it will be of lasting interest. Moreover, we have in this case no convincing scientific evidence that the movement has actually served to re-duce the level of joylessness in the general population, or in any way improved the level of contentment in corporations that have harboured it. What we have had is a series of descriptions of the theory and practice of group interaction in the professional liter-ature, a number of rhapsodic personal testimonials, and a great blaze of enthusiastic reporting in the public press. Overall, there has been a striking paucity of properly designed evaluation studies and not enough reflection on the hazards that might result from uncontrolled application of these techniques in a large and unresisting population.

This is certainly not to say that research has not been done, or that information has not been gained that would be useful to us in predicting what the outcome will be. In fact the study of group dynamics has been proceeding since the 'thirties, and a great deal is known by now about such matters as the experimental creation of social norms, group cohesiveness, group pressures, the manipulation of group atmosphere, the nature of primary groups, spontaneous social organization, sociograms, communications in task-oriented groups, and numerous other aspects of the process. The explosive diffusion of interest in the group within the last decade has not rendered these early studies obsolete. On the contrary, it has accorded them a practical significance that did not obtain, locally at any rate, at the time the work was originally done.

Along with every other manifestation of the Counter Culture, the H.P.M. may finally be shown to be a most enlightened and necessary reaction to the dehumanizing processes of the modern industrial state. Yet it is possible to discern certain characteristics in the movement that a student of history might be inclined to describe as sinister. There are, of course, many influences in our society that tend, through mutual reinforcement, to cause discontent and a subsequent desire for radical change. It is my contention that Organization Development is now one of these influences, depending as it does for its effectiveness on the reorientation of individuals through their participation in training seminars, and also on its tendency to discredit the values of our major social institutions. Of orgment's claim to enhance organizational efficiency Campbell and Dunnette have written: "The assumption that T-group training has positive utility for organizations must necessarily rest on shaky ground. It has neither been confirmed nor disconfirmed." The real interest in O.D., however, does not lie in the possibility that it may not be positively beneficial. It lies in the possibility that it may actually be harmful. The hazards of O.D. derive from the fact that it may cause acute distress in individual cases, and also that it may undermine certain crucially important values that serve to support the free society. A Toronto industrial psychologist named David Jackson has been quoted as saying: "The Human Potential Movement calls into question some of the basic competitive assumptions of free enterprise. After he gets through sensitizing himself, an employee may decide he'd rather go off somewhere and devote his life to, say, learning the piccolo." O.D. is of particular interest here, moreover, because it operates not as an isolated agency, as does Esalen, for example, but as an integral part of the organizations of the society.

Accordingly, we must attempt to answer three questions:

Is it correct to assign O.D. a place in the human potential movement, and to identify it, by extension, as an arm of the Counter Culture?

Does the pleasing facade of O.D. indicate, in any way accurately, the nature of the structure that stands behind it?

Does O.D., in fact, tend to discredit the institutions of society? It is important, I think, for these questions to be considered. O.D. has been very successful, perhaps because its contribution to organizational excellence has been commensurate with its claims. On the other hand very few people, it would seem, have wondered whether there might be some pernicious effects on our society if the triumphant advance of O.D. is permitted to continue unchecked. If it is both worthy and benign, O.D. should be able to withstand the scrutiny of a sceptic who is as concerned about the health of the society as O.D. itself now claims to be.

The question as to whether O.D. may properly be assigned a place within the alternate society must seem perfectly absurd to many people. Even so let it be asked. If it cannot be answered in the affirmative then those of us who are admirers of the culture will be reassured. If, on the other hand, convincing arguments can be adduced that clearly align O.D. with other influences that are known to facilitate social decay then, duly warned, we may be better prepared to resist its further advance. At the very least it seems reasonable that the people who find themselves involved in it—and this is very often not a voluntary involvement—should be informed on the nature of the process that is about to become an influence in their lives. It is a matter of great importance that the prospective trainee be told precisely what social values the trainers of O.D. subscribe to, and what risks attend submission to the techniques to be used.

He will not be given any such information by his employer. He will only be told that O.D. has been carefully examined by the organization and that this has resulted in complete approval. A comprehensive programme of re-education is in the course of being implemented and this training, which began at the top, has now reached the level of what is described as "the line". As a line person, he is strongly urged to participate in this pro-gramme and to attend the week-long expense-paid seminar to be held at a centre some distance from the city. This is described as a first-phase educational programme.

Now the worker who, let us suppose, is a supervisor of some ten other people in an office, has never previously been told any-thing of consequence about O.D. There have been occasional rumours to the effect that some plan for re-organization has been started but this, after all, is a constant preoccupation of many such organizations. But this time it has been kept utterly secret that top management is deeply involved in a truly revolutionary scheme. This is what one would expect, of course, because O.D. is not something desired by the workers and demanded by them. It is something that begins near the top, secures the top, and then, over a period of several years proceeds systematically to involve people at ever lower levels within the organization. In this sense O.D. displays similarities with pyramid selling, except that the pyramid in the case of O.D. is actually started in the rarefied air of the executive suite. Recruitment in pyramid selling occurs at ground level, and this causes the structure to rise from a broadening base to a height that is limited only by the gullibility of the people. Group management is essential, however, to both.

The supervisor, then, receives a memorandum advising him that a managerial grid seminar is to be held on a certain date. The memorandum states that this seminar is for key staff who are ready to participate in Phase I of a comprehensive programme of organization development. This is followed by a brief and cryptic quotation, source not given: "The Seminars will increase your insight into your own attitudes, assumptions and values about leadership and membership in your organization. It will provide an opportunity for you to gain understanding of three key concepts: *team action, organization culture, organizational change.*"

Most of this cannot mean a great deal to the supervisor. He will conclude, however, from the high tone of the memorandum, that this is an invitation of more than routine interest. He decides to accept. He has no knowledge of the fact that, should he decline, the Personnel and Training Office would be discomfited and fall back on its repertoire of ingenious strategies for use against resisters. Everything is voluntary, except of course that the organization is committed to a programme that requires total acceptance. Moreover a great deal of money has already been spent. Resisters are expected but they cannot be tolerated indefinitely. Dissent is disharmonious, undesirable, and finally anti-social.

However, the supervisor imagines that his decision to accept the invitation is quite voluntary. He will then proceed to learn, in the course of completing his twenty hours of pre-seminar homework, that O.D. exists to help him create a more excellent organization. He will read *Corporate Excellence Through Grid Organization Development* and *Corporate Excellence Diagnosis.* He will not be exposed to a single word of caution or doubt. All the material presented to him in the course of his early indoctrination will have been carefully screened. It will all be joyously positive. O.D. will appear as free of risk and blemish as the Wesleyan Church in the 18th Century. It is simply one of those perfect systems whose virtue can be taken for granted.

It is interesting to recall that in the 18th Century in France the philosophes were concerned to destroy the *ancien régime*, replace it with an ideal system, and promote the nearly mystical idea of the natural order. The driving force of the revolution was based on the premise that the concept of the natural order was so true that it could be accepted on faith. Eventually those who did not see that this was so were identified as either criminal or insane. Any system that sanctifies itself is worth at least a brief examination. It may contain a potential for authoritarianism.

At the seminar our co-operative supervisor is told he will learn a great deal about human behaviour in organizations, and his skill in interpersonal relationships will be immeasurably improved. He can only think all this will redound to his advantage. Awareness is, after all, universally acclaimed. He will note, at some point, that the group is the fundamental unit in the organization. This will not mean much to him. There are always groups. He has worked in groups all his life. He is involved with other people in a variety of affairs both within the organization and outside of it. People often do things together and this agreeable tendency will be favoured.

He may be surprised to learn that the teaching methods of the past, directed at individual learning, had not proven of value. He imagines he has learned quite a bit in the course of his own training and experience and perhaps wonders what new teaching methods have been invented by the Centre that render so valueless those familiar to him. The brochure accompanying his application form indicates that his "creativity will be unleashed" and that his "commitment will be developed". This may be a clue to the nature of the new learning experience. Commitment had not specifically been taught before. Applying the old methods to the teaching of such a thing might well not work. The new method would teach something that was not previously on the curriculum and then, in the course of time, the new item would be assigned a greater value and the things that were once taught and the method used to teach them would, accordingly, be downgraded. It may be, thinks the supervisor, that a new system of values is apparent here. Such things as commitment and creativity will be especially honoured and even—he finds this hard to believe—specifically taught.

Let us suppose this man is an intelligent person who has gained a certain wisdom in the course of his many years in the organization. He is not really a cynic, but he has observed the frailties of men for a long time and gained some awareness of their tendency to be gullible and vulnerable to the arousal techniques of charismatic speakers. He has learned, especially, that men respond eagerly when they are promised some attribute they know they do not possess. He knows that today any source offering enhanced creativity is sure to draw thousands of people. He knows the aspirations of these people will soar, and that the gulf that separates aspiration from reality will eventually be the measure of their disappointment. Accordingly he wonders whether the Centre is justified in using the word creativity so promiscuously. In fact he is troubled by the frequent occurrence of a number of high-sounding phrases and sentences in the material given to him.

"Dynamic change process."
"The development of a dynamic, strategic model."
"Organizations of the future will be rapidly changing, temporary systems."
"Building synergetic and collaborative cultures will become essential."
"Experiential learning techniques."
"Maximize opportunities for human growth."
"The goal is change."

He continues with his pre-seminar homework and soon discovers that it is shared learnings, attitudes and feelings that form the basis for co-operation. He feels this statement could well be true, but senses uneasily that his interpretation may differ crucially from that of his prospective trainers.

The supervisor then discovers that the focus within the whole organization will be on what are described as natural sub-units. The individual is not a natural unit: not any more. The focus will be on groups of people and the purpose of the organization development seminar will be to help him to improve his group-behavioural competence, especially concerning such matters as problem solving, communicating and decision making. Now this is a very interesting statement. Decisions will be made by the group. He wonders whether this means that he, as the person most experienced and learned in his office, will be given less authority in the future, and whether his influence will be diminished until it is on a level with that of the freshest face around the table. He wonders whether such a tendency, though admirably egalitarian, places undue emphasis on inexperience, and whether this would lead to improvement in the quality of the work. He wonders whether an interest in the quality of the work will be one of those antiquated values that will be suppressed in favour of creativity and commitment. Commitment to what, he wonders?

The supervisor also wonders whether all group members will be expected to reach complete agreement on every issue. If he is just a little better informed he may wonder whether this really refers to what has been described elsewhere as collective reasoning. In any case, it would seem that everything of any consequence will be done by the group. The word "collective" continues to unsettle him, and he muses on just how far the trainers are inclined to go in that direction. He lacks any formal training in history but it seems to him that there have been quite a number of heroic experiments in collective living in the past and that they have come invariably to fearful ends.

However, the prospective trainee chides himself for being so suspicious. He must approach the seminar in a far more receptive and positive way. There is, he will remind himself, a great need in the organization for better communication. That such a complex and serious programme should be brought to his attention and actually surprise him certainly indicates that communication has been defective for some time. He does not know, of course, that the top management people in the organization have been actively engaged in O.D. for at least fourteen months. He would be astonished to learn this remarkable fact.

Desiring to be more positive, our supervisor tells himself the managerial grid seminar will be useful if it serves simply to improve communication and his own ability to get his ideas across a little more effectively in a group. He will wonder, perhaps, about the statement that the emphasis will be placed on competence in interpersonal relationships rather than any other sort of competence that he might have. His skill at performing a certain task, it would seem, is not as highly valued as his skill in relating to people. And it would seem that the latter skill is relatively defective in his case, as he has been advised to take the managerial grid course. He does not know that everyone in charge of at least one other person is considered to be a manager. All such people will eventually be advised that they are key people and that, if they are ready, the course is available to them.

Even so, there is always a great need for some improvement in interpersonal relationships. The seminar will be an enjoyable and useful experience. He will learn, he is assured, how to become more open, and how to be a more authentic human being in every way. He is not at all sure what it is to be more authentic or to have more authentic human relationships, but he concludes that mystery will be cleared up in the course of the seminar. It seems likely then that the goals of the O.D. centre are benign, and that, in departing from his usual environment, the trainee will not encounter anything so drastically alien as a branch of the alternate society.

As a rule the growth centre is far removed from the place

where the participants ordinarily live and work. It is designed to be a retreat. It is not particularly easy to reach and therefore just as difficult to escape from. The centre provides a director who is usually a resourceful and high-spirited man filled with the optimism of the H.P.M. He is a man with a mission. Old-fashioned management practices, which he sees to his horror everywhere, must be suppressed, and new fashionable practices universally introduced. The centre also presents a staff of enthusiastic converts to potentialism, most of whom are probably very modestly educated in any traditional sense. They are great at interpersonal relationships, however, and they know all about the theories espoused by the director.

Now we must remember that orgment is concerned to be respectable. Within their breasts its workers harbour the desire to be radical, and were unexampled in their adventurousness when they spent a few weeks at Esalen last year. At the centre, however, they must be considerably more restrained so as not to terrify the managers in their charge. Their stated interest is to bring about organizational change and therefore they are representative of that branch of the movement that derived originally from McGregor, the Group Relations Conferences of the Tavistock Clinic in London, and the Washington School of Psychiatry. These and eventually numerous other organizations studied not so much the individual as the group itself; then the group in its relations with progressively larger groups within an organization; and finally the interactions between organizations. The above can be described as process-centred groups. The National Training Laboratory, on the other hand, has tended to interest itself more and more intensely in what may be called individual-centred groups. The objective in such cases was to cause attitudinal reorientation in the individual members of the group. The behaviour of the entire group in relation to other groups was not of primary interest.

This distinction is not really a very useful one, however, because in actual practice both process-centred and individual-centred groups use many of the same techniques to effect personality change in individual people. They are both part of the human potential movement: examples taken from any point on its spectrum will be found to be strongly driven by the utopian urge. They are all alike in two fundamental respects: they promise a fuller realization of what is called the human potential of their clients, and they depend, for the achievement of this goal, on the promotion of group-regressive behaviour. To this end they use certain behaviour-control techniques, the T-group and its many successors, to bring about the acceptance of a new system of values. It is these techniques, as a class, that are often referred to as sensitivity training.

The supervisor is assigned a room and notes immediately that this room is to be shared by at least one other man. In fact he soon discovers that for the next week he will never be alone. Even though the setting is idyllic he will find it very difficult to go for a long walk by himself. The centre insists that people be friendly and together and fully engaged in interpersonal relating. In any case the programme is designed in such a way as to keep the participants busy all of the time. There are lectures, group discussions, film demonstrations, group outings, meals in the common dining-room and a whole series of task-oriented group activities. After the late-night bull session is over the supervisor drops into bed, quite thoroughly exhausted. In many centres the participants get only four or five hours' sleep a night and so by the end of the week fatigue becomes a very useful influence for student receptivity.

The first day will probably begin with a lecture in the old style, but as a rule such a didactic approach is soon set aside. The schoolmates are taught a very particular philosophy but the emphasis is on the nature of organizations. Of course the fearful, hierarchical, power-driven organization described by McGregor under theory X is singled out for castigation. The supervisor notes that his organization affords a good illustration of theory X. According to theory Y, a variant of which is taught at the centre, authority and obedience have no place. The supervisor is told that as a key staff member he will have to be convinced that any dynamic change process in the organization will require the co-operation of the top people. He is told that this change cannot be expected to happen overnight. Everyone will have to be re-educated. This re-education, a time-consuming process in itself, must be preceded by the development of a dynamic strategic model for the organization. Our supervisor learns now that the really top people have already spent several sessions at the centre and that orgment is being implemented in his organization in a systematic way. The session he is attending is being conducted for the education of such line people as supervisors and professional staff. From now on there will usually be at least forty staff members at the centre until everyone has been processed. At the moment what is going on is the "first phase educational programme".

The lecturer now reads a famous statement by Warren G. Bennis: "Organizations of the future, I predicted, will have some unique characteristics. They will be adaptive, rapidly changing temporary systems, organized around problems to be solved by groups of relative strangers with diverse professional skills." The supervisor considers that this statement is sheer nonsense but he immediately reminds himself that this is only the first morning. Perhaps far more sensible and practical things will eventually be said. In this he is doomed to be disappointed but for the moment he remains hopeful. He is told that in the future people will be evaluated not in a simple vertical hierarchy according to rank and status but flexibly according to competence. The aggressive, inner-directed 19th-century autocrat is dead. The supervisor recognizes the great barons of industry in this description; but he knows that these famous entrepreneurs have not been seen for years.

The lecturer now indicates that organizational development comprises a series of planned activities aimed at increasing individual and especially work-group ability to solve organizational problems and achieve organizational goals. The supervisor fails to see anything very startlingly new about that. The lecturer now indicates that the philosophy of training is constantly being examined. "The potential of training as an instrument for changing not only individuals but also the climate and operation of the entire organizational system, are being explored. The term O.D., however, refers to no formal set of techniques—there are none—but to a general point of view which may be implemented in a variety of ways. This focuses on the total organization and on natural sub-units rather than on individuals. They emphasize experiential learning techniques. The subject matter includes real problems that exist in the organization but the emphasis is placed upon competence in interpersonal relationships rather than upon task skills. Goals frequently have to do with the development of group behavioural competence in areas such as communication, decision making and problem solving. And finally they are anchored in an humanistic value which is committed to integrating individual needs and management goals, maximizing opportunities for human growth and development, and encouraging more open, authentic human relationships. The goal is change."

Now this lecture seems to the supervisor to be a marvel of jargon and cant. He is wise enough to detect the language of the doctrinaire devotee to some philosophic system or other. And he recognizes that even though the environment is rather pleasant the ideas being expressed in it are, for him, exceedingly radical. At least they imply the possibility of radicalism. There is also something disagreeably authoritarian and messianic about the style of the lecturer. He seems to be party to some great truth regarding the human condition and he is determined to make everyone join him in his naive belief. The supervisor continues to be rather doubtful about the repeated references to groups.

After lunch the afternoon session begins with the presentation of the peculiar system of personal diagnosis subscribed to by the centre. Let us suppose that in this case the director has been persuaded that the system developed by Robert R. Blake is the best of all possible instruments.

The supervisor is fascinated by this description of the Blake Managerial Grid. So are all of his colleagues. It gives an agreeably scientific impression, presenting as it does a pattern made up of nine points along the abcissa and nine along the ordinate. In fact what Blake has devised is a nosologic system comprising five main categories. It is a further transmogrification of the ancient Greek system whereby the people in the barren hills may be distinguished from the people in the fertile valleys, and of numerous other classificatory systems from Kretschner through Reich to Sheldon. This system, in its simplicity, is at least as elegant, and as useful too, as was that of the Greeks.

The students are given various questionnaires to fill out and on the basis of these they are able to plot themselves on the grid. The two dimensions differentiate between concern for production and concern for relationships. If, on the grid, the student plots himself at the lower left-hand corner then he is a 1, 1, the position representing impoverished management. He is interested in neither products nor people. He is a hopelessly bad manager who imagines that people are lazy, apathetic and indifferent. Mature relationships are impossible for this person. However if the student rises to the top of the scale on the left then he is a 1, 9, a "country club manager" for whom production is secondary to lack of conflict among people and a general spirit of good fellowship. It is amusing to realize that this manager is very similar to McGregor's theory Y, the best and most humane of all bosses. Blake rejects this overly soft-hearted manager just as he rejects the 9, 1, the completely task-oriented manager who resembles McGregor's theory X man. The middle of the road manager is said to be fair but firm. He likes people a bit and he thinks the product should also appear on the scene, but he is not excessively motivated in either of these directions. He is a 5, 5, right in the centre of the grid.

The supervisor could see this coming but now it is confirmed. The 9,9 is the ideal and this is what Blake calls "the team manager". This man believes in a perfect integration between task and human requirements. Why should the supervisor care about all this puerile plotting? He soon finds out. He is a 5,5, an insufficient worker unerringly diagnosed by the grid. And Blake is a psychologist who should know all about human personality tests. This is very unnerving. How can the supervisor possibly oppose the ideas and methods of so learned a master of psychology as Robert Blake? There is certainly something intimidating about a psychological test, no matter how simple it is, particularly for people who have had little or no experience with such things.

But these tests are not by any means the end of it or even the most important part of it. In most of these management development centres the T-group is the basic tool and the leader is described as a trainer, facilitator, expediter or change agent. All of these terms are highly revealing. The assumption is clearly made that the problems of the organization are referable to the poor capacity to relate that may be detected in the employees. If they are to become satisfactory managers they must learn the skills peculiar to the glorious 9,9 man. But they are already conditioned by the society to be interested in the product, and anyway the product is not really of much interest to the trainers. The real problem is that all these hateful, repressed and opaque people must become, for the first time in their lives, real human beings. And it is in the T-group that this miraculous change can be brought about.

For the rest of the week T-groups are held daily. They go on for several hours at a time. In spite of all the blackboard diagrams, tear sheets, questionnaires and other rather more formal events it is in the T-group that the real work is done. The rest is all display to give the impression of order, good sense, and attention to real management problems. It is in the experiential T-group that the ideal style of management is illustrated. It is utterly opposed to the design according to theory X. There is no well-defined chain of command because there is in effect no structure and no leader. There is no system of procedure because in the T-group there are no instructions to the participants other than that they should talk and relate to one another. There is no division of labour based on specialization because all the members are absolutely equal. There is no emphasis on technical competence. In the T-group the hated pyramid is flattened until it becomes a plain.

By the end of the week the supervisor has come close to being indoctrinated into the new culture, but not quite. He is confused and troubled but he has not experienced any total conversion. On the last night he is put in the hot seat. In this game one member sits in the centre of the circle and all the others produce highly emotional statements about him in fifty words or less. After all ten group members, with whom he has worked all week, have taken him apart, and he has tried to defend himself against this onslaught, he is almost ready to believe that it is all true. He really is an insufficient supervisor and he is not well liked. Particularly it hurts that these people have found so much about him that is distasteful. Disapproval by the group is a hard thing to take and he begins to desire most earnestly to learn how to learn the necessary skills in interpersonal relationships that would make him a more acceptable, even lovable, person.

And so in this troubled state he returns to the city and tries to re-enter the world that has continued to exist outside of the encampment in the wilderness. And for a great many people this is not an easy thing to do. Among numerous other vivid memories of his week at the centre, he recalls that a colleague who works on the same floor with him had weepingly revealed to the group that he had been unfaithful to his wife. That he had, in fact, had an affair with a secretary from the executive suite and that this girl had told him a number of altogether surprising things about the behaviour of the top management team.

The supervisor wondered whether this potentially damaging information could ever be passed on within the organization, or outside it to other people, including the man's wife. He wondered about all sorts of highly personal bits of information revealed in the course of the managerial grid seminars. He tried to recall what he himself had disclosed to the very colleagues from whom it had always been his policy to withhold the intimate details of his private life. He wondered, further, whether it was desirable for the top management to have all this information about the employees of the company. It seemed to him there was absolutely no way to prevent the trainers or participants from talking to anyone they wanted to. There was certainly no guarantee of professional confidentiality at the orgment centre. The trainers were not restrained by any association in some professional organization. In fact it seemed to the supervisor that orgment could be a most effective way of getting something on somebody. He mentioned this to a man from the personnel department and was told brusquely that he was just being paranoid. No records were kept, he was told; and absolutely no reports were turned in by the centre to the company. Somehow this did not seem particularly reassuring to the man who had involuntarily attended an orgment seminar.

*　*　*　*　*

J. K. Galbraith's approach to the great corporation is, of course, very different from that of Douglas McGregor. He points out that in American society the individual is constantly honoured but the committee is an object of contempt. Galbraith observes: "Admission to heaven is individually . . . ; the top management even of an enterprise with an excellent corporate image cannot yet go in as a group."

Galbraith published *The New Industrial State* in 1967 and in it he argued quite convincingly that in the great corporation everything was already being done by groups of technocrats, and that the individual had become a mythic figure who had reality only when he ran a corner variety store. I am inclined to think that in the last few years St. Peter may have entirely revised his admission policies. Today I should think that the entire management of American Airlines could arrive at the pearly gates together and be checked out as a single, and even natural, unit of consciousness.

6

The Encounter

I have suggested that Douglas McGregor was one of the founders of Organization Development but that in the end he was betrayed by the hundreds of lesser men who picked up his basic theme and debased it. With respect to the encounter, Carl Rogers stands in a somewhat similar position. Rogers was undoubtedly one of the pioneers in the small-group field and it was he who coined the phrase "basic encounter group". If anyone can be said to have invented this form it would probably be Rogers. Yet he has said: "I deplore the games and gimmicks that have come to play such a large part in many groups and the manipulation which often accompanies their use."

Rogers proposed that in psychotherapy it was essential for the worker to be trustworthy in the eyes of his client and that this required that he be "dependably real." Thus to be merely consistent was to be phoney much of the time because even such learned and well-adjusted people as psychologists must be angry at least occasionally. If they are angry or anxious or depressed then to be trustworthy they must not conceal these moods. Rogers also said: "The most basic learning for any one who hopes to establish any kind of helping relationship is that it is safe to be transparently real."

Immediately we may perceive the simple ideas that drove the encounterists who followed Rogers to excess and absurdity. If the leader is to achieve reality through emotional incontinence then it follows that the other members of the group must seek the same goal in the same way. The hordes of less qualified and less responsible people who rushed into the encounter field during the 'sixties could not possibly be content with such weak exercises as the T-group, and even Rogers' own client-centred therapy. These people felt that if the medicine was to be considered strong then it must have a strong effect on the consumer. They wanted colour and variety; they wanted the medicine to be irresistibly strong so that there would be no doubt about their own omnipotence as healers.

Rogers should have known that this would happen, but it is astounding to me how often in the history of ideas the fathers have failed to predict the antics of the sons. Rogers suggested the masks must be cracked. He put it this way: "In time the group finds it unbearable that any member should live behind a mask or a front. Polite words, intellectual understanding of each other and of relationships, the smooth coin of tact and cover-up— amply satisfactory for interactions outside—are just not good enough. . . . Gently at times, almost savagely at others, the group demands that the individual be himself, that his current feelings not be hidden and that he remove the mask of ordinary social intercourse. In one group there was a highly intelligent and quite academic man who had been rather perceptive in his understanding of others but who had revealed himself not at all. The attitude of the group was finally expressed sharply by one member when he said, 'Come out from behind the lectern, doc. Stop giving us speeches. Take off your dark glasses—we want to know YOU'." This man, Rogers explained, nearly began to weep, but the group gathered around him gently and with their sweet support he told his "tragic personal story which accounted for his aloofness and his intellectual and academic approach to life".

This description is appalling, of course, but it is nothing compared to what others in the movement have said. Here is Fritz Perls: "Any time you use the words *now* and *how,* and become aware of this, you grow. Each time you use the question *why,* you diminish in stature. You bother yourself with false, unnecessary information. You only feed the computer, the intellect. And the intellect is the whore of intelligence. It's a drag on your life."

It is the trend that is interesting. Early on, Rogers decided that well people could get better in exactly the same way sick people get well. Maslow took this point of view a considerable step forward by suggesting that while sick people got well, well people should go far beyond mere adjustment and achieve transcendence. From this came the primary urge for self-actualization that soon became a basic concept in the H.P.M. Eventually the followers of Carl Rogers and Abraham Maslow founded the American Institute of Humanistic Psychology, and Esalen was created on 62 ineffably beautiful acres at Big Sur in California. In 1962, potentialism became a cult with both a spiritual and a physical base.

When Michael Murphy was still a student at Stanford he was enormously impressed by the teaching of Frederic Spiegelberg, a professor of Eastern philosophy. Murphy conceived of the idea that Eastern mysticism must be made to harmonize with what he identified as Western pragmatism. He meditated for six or so hours a day for about ten years and even spent a year and a half in India. Then his grandmother died and left him the property at Big Sur. It included the view, a seedy hotel and a few cabins. Murphy and Richard Price, a Harvard friend who had also been turned on by Eastern philosophy, decided to hold seminars there on the doctrines of Zen Buddhism, Hinduism and a number of other Eastern religions. It is clear in retrospect that the time for the appearance of such an ashram had come. The partners sent out letters to a number of celebrated people including Aldous Huxley and Alan Watts; they accepted, and the seminars began. At first the letterhead identified the place as Big Sur Hot Springs, but by 1964 the name Esalen Institute appeared. The place was a hit, and all the most trendy people soon began to flock to its idyllic surroundings. It immediately became *the* growth centre. At this point Murphy attended a T-group session at Carmel and had a peak experience. The encounter suddenly arrived at Esalen to stay. This was clearly the American answer that had been sought. Everybody had been searching for ways to expand consciousness and achieve joy and enlightenment but here, right in Carmel, the T-group, a completely secular event, caused Mike Murphy to peak!

By 1965 Rollo May, B. F. Skinner, Carl Rogers and Bishop James Pike had made their way to Esalen, and the fabulous mix was well under way. The Esalen environment was roiling with Indian mysticism, LSD and basic encounters. There was an increasingly desperate urge to break through to new levels of consciousness before it was too late. In the following year Maslow himself arrived, and so did William C. Schutz.

Prices continued to rise and the excitement intensified. It was clear to everyone that Esalen was the place where the design of the new world was going to be hammered out. Schutz wrote *Joy,* and his flying circus of encounter leaders caused a great stir in the nation's press. Noting this instantaneous success, Schutz came up with *More Joy.* Herbert Otto struck back with *Peak Joy,* thus revealing more authentically the purpose of the movement. Shortly thereafter, however, thinkers at the Elysium Institute in Los Angeles sent out the unbeatable news that they had created a seminar entitled "Cosmic Joy". The only way they could improve on that was the way they actually did it. They offered next a course in "Advanced Cosmic Joy". In those days, of course, Oscar Ichazo had not yet surfaced. If he had been around he could have established a seminar on "Intergalactic Joy".

Richard Alpert also arrived at Esalen but he had changed his name since his early Harvard days, when in association with Timothy Leary he had done so much to popularize the use of such drugs as psilocybin and LSD. He had spent some time in India and was now known as Baba Ram Dass. Fritz Perls and Ida Rolf joined the group and so did John Lilly. By 1970 the encounter in any one of dozens of forms had become the basic behaviour-control instrument of Esalen.

The encounter groups at Esalen were intended to promote intense group interaction. Complete openness, honesty and co-operation were expected from all participants. The curriculum of what was finally described as the Free University of Esalen was composed of a variety of workshops, many group encounters, meditation, yoga exercises, massage, and certain procedures in which the entire group was gathered together for the purpose of expressing feeling through the use of the body. Michael Murphy has been quoted as saying: "Our techniques demand the total involvement of participants and, like the experience of an LSD trip, are intensely personal and extremely difficult to describe in conventional language."

The preoccupation with the East continued unabated at Esalen, but by 1970 there had been such an immense amount of press and television coverage that the managers of the place decided to actually travel East. They took the whole circus to New York for a huge three-day awareness saturation event at the Hotel Diplomat. Just about everybody who really mattered was there. Schutz conducted one of his famous microlabs and soon had all the trippy people milling blindly about the ballroom. Bernard Gunther awakened the bodies of the participants by causing them to run about with childlike abandon. About four thousand people attended the various events in this hectic demonstration of California enlightenment.

No one seemed to realize at the time that the movement had reached its dizzy zenith. Everything was flying and nothing could stop the complete humanization of the whole country. Today New York: tomorrow the world's most unauthentic state. But the success of the movement could not depend for long on the easy enthusiasm of the devotees of the avant garde. It had to affect a far wider population; and change the very motivational roots of the society.

Could this be done? Could the philosophy of radical humanism actually be caused to prevail in our society? If it could, its proponents would have to recognize that the potency of its basic instruments, the T-group and the encounter, would depend on four crucially important variables.

The personality of the subject. It is clear that every human characteristic that can be measured, however crudely, varies widely in the degree in which it occurs across a large population. Individual differences should also be expected to occur in those variables that cannot as yet be accurately quantified. The tendency to be obedient, for example, must vary widely. The tendency to be suggestible must be the same. The ability to maintain a certain point of view will vary from person to person and in the same person from time to time. In short we may assume that some people are more easily persuaded than others. Some people, accordingly, will be more vulnerable to persuasion through the techniques of the T-group and the encounter than will others. This variable may be just as significant in any consideration of these techniques as it is in any consideration of the effects of the illusionogens.

The problem that arises here is that in most cases there is no screening of the candidates for the encounter either through ignorance or intentional design. It is actually held by a number of leaders that the precipitation of a psychotic episode is of the greatest value. As a result people who are managing to function in a marginal way are sometimes caused, in the course of one of these encounters, to decompensate to the point of overt symptom formation. Again the statistics regarding this are quite inadequate. The practitioners of the movement do not, of course, collect statistics or report on the incidence of psychosis. The clinicians, on the other hand, who are called upon to treat these casualties, may well gain a distorted view of this problem. A number of them have reported high rates of serious emotional disturbance following encounter sessions, including suicide. Nor is it only in the highly charged encounter group that serious psychological disturbances can be precipitated. Even in the T-group vulnerable people have been known to have severe reactions of this type. The point here is that if the movement is to gain a strong foothold in this culture it must depend on the recruitment of those who feel most alienated and discontented. Among these people it needs the support of those most vulnerable to persuasion. Let there be casualties: the society will just have to pay this price for its salvation.

The personality, training and skill of the leader. This, of course, is one of the most worrisome problems in the whole area. It would seem anyone can offer his services as a trainer and as long as ten or so people recognize him as such he will be in business. People who have attended a few encounter sessions are especially liable to conclude that they are peculiarly suited to assume the role of trainer. There are no controls over them. Advertisements in the *Village Voice,* for example, have stated quite simply that a particular person would be available for awareness training on a certain date at a certain place. No professional training or experience is necessary because no treatment is offered. The charge that the trainer is practising therapy under false pretences is entirely obviated in this way. A normal person is simply offering to interact with a group of unselected normal people. As a matter of fact many practitioners now hold that a professional degree is a positive handicap to leadership. William C. Shutz, one of the most widely publicized exponents of the encounter, has said that psychiatrists make the worst leaders and that psychologists and social workers are only slightly better. Any sort of academic training inhibits the leader. Such a person is too intellectual and this prevents him from being spontaneous and human. In the movement the intellect is always finally the enemy. The ideal leader is warm, innocent, and tender; and he has no professional facade to hide behind.

There are no state or provincial standards or ethical requirements that might regulate this field. The self-appointed expediter or facilitator is apparently well defended against lawsuits because he does not hold himself out as a person offering treatment of any kind. There is, of course, no professional society anywhere of encounter-group practitioners. Such societies ordinarily attempt to establish minimal standards of training and conduct in their respective fields. There are no such minimal standards in the human potential movement and this includes the practitioners of the T-group, the encounter group and of organization development. The National Training Laboratory in Washington, it is true, has interested itself in this question, and states in its manual *Standards for the Use of Laboratory Method*: "No capability as a T-group trainer or consultant should be assumed as a result of participation in one or more basic laboratories or other short-term experiences." It must be recognized, however, that the N.T.L. now plays a relatively small role in the expanded universe of the movement. This nascently conservative position on the part of the N.T.L. does not guide the numerous other groups employing the same techniques. Furthermore the N.T.L. has no actual control over the behaviour of its graduates once they complete their training.

The personality, experience and skill of the trainer are usually quite unknown to the people who place themselves in his charge. His influence, it seems to me, will then be determined at least in part by the relative strength of his personality vis-a-vis the personality of each member of the group. Some people might be overwhelmed by him and made obedient and suggestible; others might be extremely resistant. The encounter-group leader seems to play the same role in his area as does the guru in the drug using subculture. In both cases the influence of the guide may be crucially important in causing attitudinal reorientation in his followers. They are the shamans of the modern industrial state; and they may have assumed a power far greater than anyone imagines.

Throughout history, and in every part of the world, leaders of political, ideological and religious systems have played roles of critical importance not only in the process of conversion but also in the continuing guidance of the believers so created. It would be unreasonable for us to conclude that the leader, in any of his protean forms, has now lost his ancient power. It is quite impossible at this point to determine the actual extent of the influence wielded by our encounter leaders. For one thing their essential philosophic position tends to result in fragmentation and bitter internecine hostility. This probably has served to reduce their impact on society. They have, many of them, simply burnt themselves out, or been so furiously innovative, that they have found themselves on ground too insufficiently firm to attract more than the most gullible of people. In such cases they have suffered the fate of all explosive faddists.

Typically, encounter leaders are arrogant men who are never themselves satisfied with the status quo. They will always be urged to extend their influence as they come to sense it. When one technique begins to seem passé then it is revised, through a series of steps, until it reaches an extreme form. The trainer and his followers are impelled in the same direction, and each step removes them that much further from the continuing life of the inclusive society. Re-entry is particularly difficult for the true habitué of the drug or the encounter experience.

The third variable concerns the value system that prevails in the milieu. It tends to be established by the trainer, of course, but he himself belongs to a group of like-minded trainers and the growth centre itself will undoubtedly present a system of values that can be described. This system is ordinarily very similar to that typical of the alternate society. It is especially evident in places like Esalen but even in the most apparently conservative growth centres the collectivist impulse is very strong.

The movement, it would seem, is always radical in nature. Its driving force derives from emphasis on change and this, it must be agreed, consistently stimulates it to attack everything that is conservative in the culture. Convulsing as it is with its fascination for novelty and its conviction of sanctity, the movement pushes itself with each new spasm towards an ever more extreme position on the left. This is inevitable. The tendency is an integral part of any millennial movement, and the encounter culture is such a movement today.

We may observe then that if the movement is to be successful it must affect those who are most easily persuaded, it must use charismatic leaders, and it must present a reasonably well-integrated philosophy that appears to be novel and useful. To people inclined to disaffection the ideas of the Counter Culture can be immensely appealing. But these variables might not be sufficient in themselves to bring about the necessary change. The movement must make use of techniques potent enough to affect at least some people who are not among the most easily persuaded in the population. The techniques are not more important than the general willingness to be persuaded, the power of the leaders, and the radical philosophy, but they are essential nevertheless.

The techniques employed in the human potential movement range from mild discussion to some very exotic and physically dangerous practices. It must be obvious that the potency of the techniques will depend on the degree to which the subjects can be caused to surrender their individuality and immerse themselves in the consciousness of the group.

The encounter group uses a wide range of verbal and non-verbal exercises. Direct verbal exchange is most commonly promoted and in such cases every degree of violence short of the physical is ordinarily allowed. Though the Counter Cuture claims to despise striving it may still be observed that there is much striving for openness and candour in the encounter group. The member who is instructed to punch his fist into a pillow and shout, "I hate you," is usually derided by the others for his failure to be sufficiently expressive and authentic in his rage. He is made to repeat this exercise over and over again until he gets it right. It is *de rigueur* to state precisely, in the most direct fashion, what one feels about everything and everybody.

Very often games that permit the expression of actual physical aggressiveness are engaged in. Thus Indian wrestling is common and sometimes actual wrestling is promoted. Various other kinds of physical intimacy are also permitted and some of these are intentionally sexual in nature. Rocking, restraining, dancing, hugging, kissing, spreadeagling and eyeballing are commonly used techniques. Everything is done, it is said, to increase awareness and stimulate emotional attitudes. A session may begin, for example, by the expediter encouraging everyone to scream as loudly as possible. Since uninhibited screaming is not condoned in society after the age of four this produces in the participants a contagious sense of abandon. The people may then be instructed to flap their arms and jump up and down for a few minutes. Again disinhibition is promoted as everyone obediently complies. Such vigorous exercises are commonly alternated with periods of repose. Thus the subjects are caused to move from sensory over-stimulation to sensory deprivation. Meditation is an important device of the encounterists, as are a number of oriental exercises such as yoga. This may be followed by hand touching and hugging. The leader, throughout all this, assumes a progressively more omnipotent position despite his protestations to the contrary. The people are progressively more suggestible.

The group may then be instructed to make direct confessions. Only the person who is completely open will gain the admiration of the leader and of the group. He who retains any secret will be identified as deviant. It is necessary to give up one's individuality and let one's self be swallowed up by the group. There is no other way short of departing from the scene. If this is a procedure arranged by one's employer, as is the case with organization development, departure may not seem to be advisable.

The game of break-in and break-out may then be played. In this, one person is asked to force his way into a circle of his comrades who have locked their arms and legs together. Minor physical injuries often occur in such games because people tend to play them with altogether astonishing degrees of ferocity.

The leader may now say: "Somewhere in this room there is a place where you will feel comfortable. Discover where that place is." The enthusiastic game players begin to search all over the room and finally they find their perfect places. If anyone should say he was comfortable where he was he would be chided by the group. If the place was to be found by searching then this procedure must be carried out. Obviously it is not the finding of the place that counts; it is the following of the manipulative order to find that place.

The expediter may now instruct the adults in his command to ooze to the floor and spread around in the manner of an invertebrate animal. After this difficult anatomical trick is successfully completed the instructor may point out that his charges in fact have backbones. They all make this discovery for themselves, and it is very exhilarating. The instructor notes that they can even crawl, and they all begin to prove this astonishing truth by crawling, eyes shut, all over the room. The instructor now advises the mature social workers, psychologists and teachers that they could even walk on all fours if they wanted to. I think the reader will recognize here that this absurd little exercise is designed to recapitulate the entire phylogenetic history of man, but only according to the limited understanding of this subject of the trainer.

The trainer now suggests that his rapidly evolving creatures could even stand on two legs, in the manner of chimpanzees. The discovery of this capability strikes the participants as altogether refreshing and they proceed to leap and lurch about the room with their long arms dangling almost to the ground and with their jaws underslung to the extent that, as human beings, they are capable. These primates are now told to open their eyes and notice the presence of other equally developing animals of a similar species. And indeed there are real social workers and teachers all over the room pretending to be apes. These beasts are told to cluster in small groups and hug one another; and on so doing they achieve the highest level. They are human beings. Now all that remains is for them to become sensitive human beings. They have yet to realize their full potential.

The wretched subjects may be asked to converse with each other in gibberish or play some vaguely psychological version of charades, or finger paint, or perform somersaults, or go for a blind walk. In this last exercise one person is blindfolded and he is led by a second person all over the building or onto the lawns of the retreat. In this way, it is believed, he learns to trust another person. A similar game involves one person falling backwards into the catching arms of the group.

William C. Schutz has described dozens of these little games in his several books. With respect to one member of the group the others are asked to say what colour he would be if he were a colour, what piece of furniture if he were a piece of furniture, what part of the body, what smell, what animal? etc. There is no end to innovation. Schutz writes: "The unwillingness to display one's self in front of others, as in public singing, is a major deterrent to free expression." Accordingly he orders the seeker after free expression to sing before the group. Everyone is very tolerant of this and applauds at the end. I can assure the reader that if a trained and gifted singer should render an aria from *Don Giovanni* he would be vigorously scorned and described as a phoney and elitist showoff. All people are equal and therefore all people should sing publicly and be applauded—except serious professionals who tend to make everyone else feel inferior.

Schutz sometimes tells people that for a particular session no words at all will be allowed. Everyone must relate non-verbally. Schutz observes: "This was a unique experience. The group danced, gestured, played footsie, acted out meanings, and did many other things. One surprising discovery became apparent. It seemed that a much clearer picture emerged of each of the group members after the wordless first meeting than ordinarily exists after a more traditional first meeting. Perhaps this discovery underscores the use people make of words to prevent others from knowing them."

Blind milling is one of Schutz' favourite devices. In this exercise everyone is instructed to stand up, close eyes, extend hands, and start milling about the room. He advises his people to explore each other whenever they accidentally touch. He thinks this method enhances cohesive ties within the group and sharpens awareness of other people as human beings. He also says he sometimes begins groups by having each member stand before the others. The members comment briefly on what they see. They then walk up and touch the specimen. They are ordered to feel the texture of his skin, the tone of his muscles. They are asked to push him and note the amount of resistance this produces. "Now smell him", says Schutz and everyone has a good long smell of this man before they make their final judgement on him.

Also at the beginning of a group Schutz points out that all the members have names, occupations and histories of one sort or another. He says all these things get in the way of authenticity. The group, accordingly, will examine each member in turn and assign names, occupations and assorted other details that serve, ordinarily, to identify a person. Sometimes the group assigns women's names to certain men whom they regard as being a bit effeminate, but the assigned name tends to stick for the duration of the seminar. Occasionally an especially co-operative member will be reconsidered later on and have his name changed from Felicity to Rock, a decision accompanied by much rejoicing and weeping.

Schutz observes: "Especially with intellectual people, words paradoxically can be the largest obstacle to communication . . . relieving people of the burden of using words allows the real feelings to surface." In order to overcome this problem Schutz puts two people at the opposite ends of the room and tells them to advance toward each other. On meeting they are to do whatever occurs to them to do. This usually results in what has been described as "the Esalen hug", but it may also result in "the Esalen sideswipe" and a variety of other stereotyped and phoney responses. "We spent about five minutes pushing each other around the room, ending with a spontaneous, warm embrace. Our relationship therefore was indeed one between equals."

Now this is an interesting statement because the participants in this particular pushing match included the leader, William C. Schutz, Ph.D., himself.

Schutz is really a remarkable man. In *Here Comes Everybody* he instructs those of his readers who have studied less physiology than has he that "the circulation (heart) and reproduction (genital) systems are most directly related to the area of affection." This, I should think, must represent another of his important discoveries. He says further that "the honesty revolution of which encounter groups are a central part is a revolution against the fabric of our society." Sometimes he writes rather infuriating stuff. For example, he says: "My silent generation was much more prone to believe you can't fight City Hall, and to let it go at that." In 1973 Schutz is about fifty. About twenty years after he was born his silent generation was engaged in battles in the Pacific and in North Africa that were more terrible even than those at City Hall. Schutz's interest in history is as selective as is his interest in anatomy and physiology. According to Jane Howard: "Schutz dislikes secrets the way gardeners dislike weeds. He has professed to see no serious harm in a leader's sleeping with one of his own group members, provided it is for her own good and provided the leader didn't make a secret of it." The moral infraction, then, is the keeping of the secret. This attitude is precisely the one that I noted earlier at kibbutz Bittania.

In their pursuit of total openness and honesty, encounter leaders have invented some very ingenious tricks. In his couples group, for instance, Schutz asks each of the couples "to think of three secrets that they have never told their mate and that would be most likely to jeopardize the relationship". He tells us that the commonest secret is adultery but that homosexual affairs and assorted other unpleasantnesses are common enough. He notes that these revelations often engender a certain amount of anger. The really interesting thing about these confessions is that they are identical with those that are encouraged in the May 7 cadre groups in China. There is only one difference and that is in the ideological position of the group. In China the revelation of adultery, for example, would result in the collective diagnosis of poor political health, and he who revealed this crime would be encouraged to reform. At Esalen no such admonition would be issued by the group. They would all understand that such things happen and that they indicate that the couple has not been sufficiently open in the past. The ideology of total permissiveness would be promoted instead. In fact Schutz himself sets forth a poignant little story in his book. In referring to his own relationship to a woman he reveals that early on they decided to allow "outside sexual adventures": "She did it first. She came in one night and announced that she had screwed John. I then had my first experience of non-congruence between thought and feeling, head and body."

Paul Bindrim has achieved a certain notoriety by conducting much-publicized Nude Sensitivity Training workshops. Bindrim has said: "Clothing means we really don't trust each other. There's so much bullshit about an American's house being his castle, and such a fetish about privacy. After all you were born nude, weren't you?"

Accordingly Bindrim runs marathon encounters with everybody in the nude. The movie he made of such an affair was filmed in Toronto in 1970. Bindrim recruited a group of people, mostly actors, a crew of cameramen and technicians, and built a set in a film studio comprising a living room and a swimming pool connected by a short corridor. For this excursion into total authenticity Bindrim had 20 microphones hidden here and there, 9 concealed cameras, and three shifts of cinematographers. The marathon went on for 36 hours and all the time the machinery recorded everything the 18 players said and did. Everything was orchestrated to deliver up to the cutting room the very most sensitive record of the intimacy training for which Bindrim is famous. The water temperature was perfectly controlled, the piped-in music was as carefully chosen as Muzak, except that Muzak is too timid to thunder in a vast resonating human heartbeat. There were underwater strobe lights, dry ice to flood the environment with mystery, candlelight, and a lot of group chanting. All this was not enough, of course. The people were still inhibited. There was only one trick left in Bindrim's mighty bag: total, even frontal, nudity.

Finally the 36 hours were mercifully cut to 90 minutes and called *Out Of Touch*. In summing up its report on this work a local magazine said: "The actors may have played roles, as everyone does, but they could not cover up their true emotions. Restricted."

Bindrim has written: "These spontaneous excursions into nudity seem to increase interpersonal transparency. . . ." Alexander Lowen, another contributor to this form, has observed: "Nakedness is the great leveller of social distinctions for it reduces all persons to the common bodily or animal level on which they came into the world. Nudity strips the individual of his ego pretensions and, sometimes, of his ego defences . . . Nudity removes all privacy and reduces all pride."

It is Bindrim, however, who will be remembered for his single-handed refinement of the technique that had been called, for some time, "eyeballing". In eyeballing, two members of the group are caused to stare glazedly into each other's eyes for extended periods of time. Bindrim's development of this technique was called crotch-eyeballing and as such it was used to assist in the bringing about of the "peak experience" which he has claimed occurs in eighty per cent of his marathons. The joy seeker in this case places his or her bottom on a sofa cushion and lies back on the floor. Bindrim grabs the legs, lifts them high, and spreads them widely. A great mirror is then placed in front of the hapless seeker and he is instructed to regard his perineum and assorted other parts in some detail. In due course the other participants are invited to peer over Bindrim's shoulder so that they too may benefit from what may be seen there. Eventually most of the participants are accorded the opportunity of having their own crotches eyeballed and of seeing exactly what it is that all the other trainees have been hiding for all this time.

If this technique seems to the squeamish reader to suffer somewhat from a certain clinical aspect then he will be further disappointed on hearing of its further development by none other than William C. Schutz. In groups for couples, says he: "We often ask the men to use a speculum to examine the interior of the vagina." Schutz insists that "to look and see can be a very rewarding and delightful experience." He then rather plaintively observes: "I found as I was writing this last part that I was debating whether or not to include it on the basis of offending some people or giving fuel to critics." He may be right. His critics, always on the alert for inanity, vulgarity and other signs of the Communist Plot, were certain to come upon this innocent genito-urinary diversion. I wonder, though, whether Dr. Schutz has ever looked at an eardrum with an otoscope. If not, then I can highly recommend this delightful experience.

Anyway, the secret is out and Schutz has been famous for some time for his introduction of the gynecological speculum into the human potential movement. Adam and Eve were not ashamed until they ate of the Tree of Knowledge. Knowledge is a very dangerous thing in the encounter movement, and therefore if paradise is to be regained, Adam and Eve must once again be naked and unashamed.

By now there are hundreds of encounter games and just as many ancillary techniques that also claim to enhance sensitivity and promote growth and self-actualization. Awareness techniques have included some novel exercises that would have dismayed G. I. Gurdjieff, the spiritual founder of the sensory awareness movement. In 1917, Thomas de Hartmann described the master's early work with "sacred gymnastics". "There was one exercise in which the men had to fall in a heap and squirm around like snakes in a tangle of arms and legs. Suddenly Mr. Gurdjieff would cry, 'Stop' and take someone aside to let him view the group." And again: "Mr. Gurdjieff gave us some new exercises, in one of which we were given special movements for arms and legs, that stood for letters of the alphabet. We practised these for a week; then suddenly Mr. Gurdjieff announced that within the Institute we were to speak only by means of these movements."

Fifty-six years later a leader in sensory awareness training may say to the group: "Now I want you to write your names with your shoulder blades". The room is soon filled with heaving shoulder blades. The people are then instructed to see a finger, smell it, feel it, or just generally groove on this thing that they had presumably never experienced to the full before.

Body manipulation has produced a few curious techniques. Dr. Ida Rolf is no doubt the most celebrated contributor to this field. She has developed a technique known as Structural Integration or Rolfing which is a strange blend of massage, chiropractic, and potentialism. Rolf claims that her incredibly severe manipulations are designed to stretch the fascia and the connective tissue between the muscles, skin and bone. Only in this way can a person's body be realigned, and without such realignment joy and enlightenment are impossible. Rolfers go further: they claim to heal everything from haemorrhoids to ulcers.

The practitioners of bioenergetics believe that if you change the way the body moves and reacts then there will be a concomitant change in the mental condition of the supplicant. Following the work of Alexander Lowen, bioenergetic people instruct their clients to beat pillows and scream even as they are being manipulated physically by the therapist. This is a peculiar variety of physiotherapy with an absurdly psychological element thrown in to further disinhibit the client and prepare him, therefore, for the peak experience that will cure him of his maladies.

Bioenergetics is a further development of the entirely discredited work of Wilhelm Reich, once a student of Freud. Reich became convinced that the orgasm was the source of the life force and therefore, if a patient was to be cured, he must learn to experience the perfect orgasm. This was difficult to bring about and so Reich invented the Orgone Energy Accumulator or orgone box. And this device was used by him to cure cancer and assorted psychosexual disorders.

John Pierrakos, one of the foremost bioenergeticists of today, talks to groups of people about the blue aura of energy that surrounds everyone. This aura should flow in an harmonious figure of eight around the body but if it is blocked then all sorts of mischief follows. Fortunately bioenergeticists understand the problem. It is the insufficient production and distribution of orgone energy. They also have the answer. They advise people to vibrate their pelves and loudly shout such remarkable expressions as "Mama" and "Don't touch me." After half an hour or so of this extraordinary business the people lock their arms in a circle and experience the new energy running properly throughout their bodies and around the group.

Role-playing games include several varieties. The psychodrama of J. L. Moreno is still used, but it is the gestalt therapy of Fritz Perls that is most popular at the growth centres. Perls and his followers insist that all the trouble is due to the persistence of fragments in the memory. These must be revealed by the client while he is in the hot seat. He mentions that he has a pain in the back. "Be your back," says Perls: "What does your back say?"

At all growth centres the guided fantasy is also a favourite technique. The trainer says: "Imagine you are going into a long tunnel and at the end there is a point of light. Tell us your further experience." The subject then daydreams himself into a complicated story, and all the time he is exhorted to keep it in the here and now, reporting especially on his feelings.

One of the most extraordinary of all encounters is the technique known as the Synanon Game. This is really where the expression gut-level encounter was first applied; and that is not much of a misnomer. Synanon is a self-contained community of ex drug addicts with its base in California. I recall observing a Synanon Game in Santa Monica, and it was indeed a savage affair. The group was leaderless, although several people present had obviously been involved in numerous other games and by virtue of seniority might have been expected to have some particular influence on the group. They did not do this quite intentionally. The group swung its attention to one participant after another and systematically reduced him to the condition of a gurgling nonentity.

One youth of about 18 seemed to me especially vulnerable. He was tall and gangling, had a fair crop of acne and was obviously quite uncomfortable in the group. He lacked the savoir faire of the more experienced players and particularly lacked their verbal facility and ability to handle expletives as though they were ordinary parts of speech. The group finally got around to this silent boy and charged him right off the top with being a latent homosexual. They said they imagined he was really in love with his mother. In fact they knew no more about this boy than did I. He was new to the group. Within five minutes he was described as a crybaby and a closet queen. He was assured that he spent all of his waking hours either masturbating or thinking about masturbating. He had no guts. He was tall and ugly. He was an absolute nothing, a creature with no possible significance. But this is what the Synanon Game is like. No defence is allowed: total confession is required. The players of the game are rendered utterly transparent. But there is a most important difference between this game, rolfing, and the Schutzian microlab. The encounters at Synanon and at Daytop Village in New York are for ex heroin addicts. The stakes are therefore very high. If they fail at Synanon they will be thrown out to return to the street and begin again their excruciating lives as junkies. The woman who is rolfed at Esalen is a schoolteacher from Des Moines and if she has a finger thrust into her vagina so that the fascia of that region may be released she is at least a victim for whom failure will merely involve her returning to her second-grade class in Iowa. Perhaps this is why the Synanon Game seems so desperate and intense. The people there have a lot more to lose.

In fact Synanon is a communal place and it is astoundingly similar to the May 7 cadre schools of China. It is utterly authoritarian and its coercion is based on life or death, co-operation or lethal ostracism.

Synanon took the concept of the marathon encounter one step further. At Esalen marathons frequently went on for several days running so that the resistance of the participants would be further reduced by fatigue. At Santa Monica the Synanon Stew was invented. In this the personnel of the encounter group would be continually changing. Someone would drop in for a day or so and someone else would leave. In this way the Stew could be kept going for months and always there would be "something happening".

All the techniques that I have described have at least one common characteristic: they tend to disinhibit. They offer a licence to the participants to engage in behaviour not ordinarily condoned in adult society. It is the belief of the encounterists that the breaking of a taboo will release a person from the restraint that is binding his human potential. Therefore they encourage the breaking of taboos for precisely the same reason that the practitioners of the black arts reverse every ritual of the church. Such behaviour is unusual, and regarded by the leaders as desirable for this reason. In the movement, innovation and abandon are confused with creativity, and in this way the very meaning of the word creative is debased. If flapping one's arms, screaming uncontrollably, and hitting a pillow are creative acts, and if everyone can do these things, then everyone is *ipso facto* creative, and again the movement is collectively correct.

Furthermore all these surprising techniques can be conducted by anyone. They specifically do not require discipline or training and therefore the movement has proven, yet again, one of its own truths. Charlatans cannot be distinguished from learned men except in so far as the latter may be restrained from bringing about the general state of abandon that is required for self-actualization.

And finally these techniques all tend to advance the participants in the direction of transcendence. To this end they make use of sensory bombardment, sensory deprivation and the induction of various physiological abnormalities through hyperventilation, breathholding, and fatigue.

The people, as we know, are inclined to be obedient and suggestible to begin with. The strong and determined leader makes use of potent techniques that are designed to enhance these normal tendencies. And finally a peculiar blend of anarchism and hedonism is promoted that causes at least some people to seriously question their values, beliefs and sentiments. In short these people, far from being helped to feel less disoriented in the world, are caused to feel more insecure about themselves and more doubtful about the merits of the liberal democratic society to which they must return.

7

The Casualty Rate

During the decade of the spectacular expansion of the movement, 1962-72, there were few restraints on it: indeed it was
one of its basic principles that it should tolerate no restraint.
During this same period the media coverage of the movement
was florid and continuous, and its message was spread very
widely across the world. The HPM was surprising, often shock-
ing, and it made excellent copy. People could deplore its excesses
or they could applaud its dynamism: but either way it was
worth discussing. It seemed to reflect the spirit of the age, and
as such it was an institution with which any person could
measure his commitment to modernity. It was an explosion of the
new culture and the new culture, it was widely held, was destined
to prevail.

But apart from the fact that it attracted those desirous of
being right up to the minute in all things cultural, it made certain
claims that were bound to attract a far larger population. The
movement in all of its forms, from the T-group to the nude
marathon, claimed to enhance a sense of well-being.

People who are constantly hungry, physically sick, or burdened with labour from daylight to dusk, are not available for rolfing. Those who do relatively light work in the morning and afternoon, and who have the evenings and weekends off, can break in and break out to their hearts' content. Such people are able to go beyond the struggle for physical survival. They can contrive to make their lives more varied.

Now obviously millions of such people play golf, study bird-watching, attend the movies, read *The Decline and Fall of the Roman Empire,* take courses in potting, study the culture of the Ming Dynasty, travel to Spain, or do hundreds of other things that are novel, diverting, and stimulating. But in spite of everything the state of well-being is not quite as perfect as it should be. People still experience periods when they are depressed, anxious, and angry. They still feel lonely and powerless and alienated: not all of the time, but often enough to know that they do not enjoy these states of being. And then along comes a movement that offers to bring about tranquillity and a whole new level of awareness and sensitivity. Two large groups of people are immediately alerted: those who are emotionally distressed, and those who consider themselves well, but would like to achieve a higher level of consciousness. In the case of the second group it is not so much that the people are sick as that they are positively interested in a new life experience. Presumably this experience is not expected to reform their previous life-style so much as to enrich it. The problem here, of course, is that our society is one in which sensory overstimulation is characteristic. There is some evidence that many people are attracted to encounter groups because they are fatigued through overstimulation. They are bored, and nothing seems to excite them. The movement promises to awaken their refractory senses. It will revivify the man who is jaded through having lived in the highly charged environment of the city. And indeed, personal testimonials commonly note that boredom has been dispelled. The encounter group creates a degree of euphoria that may persist for some time after the event. This leads to at least two interesting consequences. There may be a longing for the psychic stimulation of the group and a tendency, therefore, to crave this experience. This is extraordinarily analogous to the process of drug habituation. And secondly there may be very real re-entry problems when the subject attempts to adapt to the uncompromising world that persists beyond the group.

Some published reports of encounter group success were absolutely rhapsodic. Bach, for example, reported on four hundred group members saying that "ninety per cent of these marathon group participants . . . have evaluated their 24-40 hour group encounters as 'one of the most significant and meaningful experiences of their lives'." Any technique as potent as this deserves close scrutiny. When 90 per cent of the participants speak in superlatives it is not appropriate to be merely sceptical.

Many people, however, were not sceptical and flooded in increasing numbers to the gurus who offered them self-realization and the marvellous expansion of their human potential. In the 19th Century itinerant medicine men and root doctors preyed on similarly large numbers of gullible people seeking to ameliorate their physical and psychic distress. These charlatans were eventually restrained by the Pure Food and Patent Medicine Laws passed early in this century. Today the descendants of these dynamic healers have discovered that people still suffer from loneliness, depression, anger, impotence and anxiety and that anyone can set himself up as a mind doctor. Indeed we have now entered the era of pop psych, just as certainly as the 19th Century was the era of pop physick. And the field is wide open for the audacious entrepreneur.

The private citizen today can buy the Optokinetic Learning Device, the Altered State of Consciousness Induction Device, and the Bio-Feedback Device; he may engage in any number of half-revived oriental techniques such as yoga, transcendental meditation, Tai-Chi Chuan, and Aikido; he may apply to a variety of human growth centres for gestalt therapy, basic group encounters, Structural Integration, weekend marathons, nude encounters, and a great diversity of personal growth, personal awareness and human potential groups. The point is that during the 'sixties it was widely discovered that anyone could legally counsel people or operate as a therapist without training, experience or even an ethical intent. The peak experience was offered and a great many people decided that a little discomfort might well be endured for so massive a reward.

The second claim of sensitivity training was as reductive as the first. The T-group and its many variations would bring about an enhancement of interpersonal skills. And again a vast population was aroused. Everyone wanted to be able to communicate more freely, more effectively. He who could be skilful in his relations with others would not only be more popular, he would also be more powerful. And for great corporations this promise indicated modernity, better public relations, more comfortable and therefore more compliant employees. In every way this claim was a dazzling one and few could resist it. Few, at any rate, saw that very real hazards might inhere in the techniques to be used. For many years there were absolutely no well-designed studies available that might have been used to confirm or disconfirm the claims of the encounterists.

The great leaders from Esalen to the most apparently restrained orgment retreat were regularly claiming that the incidence of both psychological and physical injury was exceedingly slight. N.T.L. director Leland Bradford reported that 0.03 per cent of the 30,000 or so people who had participated in N.T.L. laboratories had become disturbed. Severe emotional troubles continued to be reported by individual health workers but none of these served to diminish the unbounded optimism of the potentialists. They tended to ignore these reports of depression, anxiety, and suicide, and concentrated instead on the exquisite delights of sensory awareness and the peak experience. Anyone insensitive enough to criticize the movement was immediately dismissed as a hopeless reactionary. It was held that one could not possibly measure the benefits of sensitivity training, the release from inhibiting traditions, the espousal of values that would enable a person to survive in the rapidly changing world, the dispelling of loneliness and, of course, the fullest possible exploitation of the human potential of the participants. Although the information began to spread that there were at least five serious problems at Bethel each summer, N.T.L. continued to insist that there had only been 25 psychotic breakdowns among the 11,000 people in its summer programmes over a 22-year period. N.T.L. said further that in thirteen years of work with organizational development in industry 3,000 people had been dealt with, but only eight had required the services of a psychiatrist. In 1971, Stone and Tieger of the University of Cincinnati observed that there was absolutely no screening of candidates for the T-group and that this seemed to result in a rather high number of mental problems. They noted the lack of training among the leaders and wondered whether these people could recognize serious trouble and cope with it. These workers decided to examine candidates for the T-group and specifically screen out those who had particular difficulties with impulse control and reality testing, as well as those with psychosomatic symptoms. A local church was sponsoring a week-long T-group seminar and it was agreed to let Stone and Tieger screen the participants. Fifteen people were excluded from the programme but there were two dis-ruptive psychotic reactions anyway. That is a casualty rate of about two per cent after quite careful screening. These same workers did not screen 41 people attending a similar T-group seminar, and of these four, or about ten per cent, had serious psychological difficulties. This study did not have any apparent effect on the rising potentialist wave and Carl Rogers continued to talk about a casualty rate of much less than one per cent. Along with all other advocates of the form and futurism in general, he continued to say that in a highly mobile, high-density society it was necessary for people to be able to make strong and effective relationships quickly and intensely, and to be able just as easily to relinquish them. In any case, encounterists argued, their techniques were benign, and treatment with them was a prerequisite for survival on Buckminster Fuller's Spaceship Earth.

The learned societies were very slow to react to the problem posed by the group, partly because some of their most vociferous members were among the enthusiastic proponents of the new therapies, partly also because they were very sensitive to the charge of being stodgy and old-fashioned and that they, the psychological and psychiatric associations, were exceptionally fine examples of the very elitist and intellectual attitudes the groupists had said must be destroyed.

The American Group Psychotherapy Association, an organization that had been doing excellent work in its own field for many years, observed: "Small, intensive, human groups automatically facilitate superego regression, reduce ego defences, potentiate id impulses, and can be stressful to the point of producing casualties from depression, anxiety, and paranoid states, psychosis, and self-destructive acting out." The A.G.P.A. also said: "Residential, sequestered, crash groups can be an unhealthy retreat or defence against resolving day to day problems in living." And further: "There is a conspicuous anti-rational tendency among the proponents of the many crash group methods, with the implication that anyone of good will and enthusiasm can be a helpful leader."

Many people began to point out that the leaders at growth centres and orgment retreats were not guided by the rules of medical licensure or the regulations of the various psychological associations. The controversy continued. Encounterists emoted about the super humanity of the intense emotional experience. Their gimmicky techniques multiplied and became more and more ritualistic. And they talked all the time about therapy for normals and about having found the solution to alienation and existential despair. More and more they became gurus; medicine men no doubt, but especially spiritual leaders in an age of secularism and discontent. The strange thing was that the T-group and encounter leaders were restrained neither by ordination nor licensure in one of the healing professions. Such a leader was a mixture of both of these but he was not bound by their respect for responsibility.

For a long time these shamans seemed to have a perfect defence against all possible attacks. If their critics drew attention to their incompetence and illegitimacy as healers they could refer exultantly to the abundant evidence of spiritual reclamation among their parishioners. If on the other hand the critics attacked them for their irrational shamanism they could dazzle them with a mass of impressive words from the language of psychology and sociology. The leader could in fact produce a never-ending line of people ready to testify that they had been saved. These same leaders were extraordinarily lacking in awareness when it came to observing that a great many people were also being hurt. Either they did not see these people or else they concluded that the benefits to the many justified the injuries to the few. In any case the messianic urge was very strong in most potentialists, and like all revolutionaries they were convinced that their work was essential for mankind.

Morris Parloff, in his excellent critique of the small group field, said that there was an "increasing incidence of physical injury—contusions, strains, sprains, and broken limbs—as a consequence of uninhibited expressions of feeling". He asked two basic questions: are the stated goals achieved, and what are the dangers and negative effects? With respect to the further claim that orgment enhanced organizational efficiency Campbell and Dunnette concluded: "The assumption that T-Group training has positive utility for organizations must necessarily rest on shaky ground." The American Psychiatric Association's Task Force Report on Encounter Groups said: "There have been many instances of participants suffering physical injuries; some encounter group leaders focus on the mobilizing and expression of rage, and physical fights between participants who have long suppressed rage are encouraged."

In fact by the early 'seventies every clinician had seen

numerous casualties whose injuries, psychic or physical, were referable to the T-group or encounter experience. It had become extremely apparent that a well-designed study had to be carried out to determine just how great a risk was run by a participant in one of these increasingly popular exercises. In late 1968, Morton Lieberman of the University of Chicago, Irvin Yalom of Stanford, and Matthew Miles of Columbia began the first large-scale, controlled study of this field. In the next few years tantalizing facts began to emerge from their work. In 1971, they reported that the casualty rate among Stanford University students who had participated in encounter groups was ten per cent. Moreover their definition of casualty was quite strict. Yalom defined a casualty as a person who, "as a result of his encounter group experience, suffered considerable and persistent psychological distress."

For the study Lieberman et al. recruited 206 students at Stanford, all of whom wished to participate in an encounter group, and assigned them randomly to one of 17 groups led by people experienced in the encounter field. Now it is immediately possible to speculate that the Lieberman findings must be baseline ones. People who have managed to get all the way to Stanford University have already been exhaustively screened. They are not ordinary people but members of the intellectual elite of the country. They have already achieved much to qualify for admission to that university and are therefore not lacking on the whole in psychological strength and determination. Moreover their participation was entirely voluntary. In both of these regards Lieberman's subjects differ strikingly from the members of an accountancy department at some midwestern manufacturing company who are all persuaded willy-nilly to spend time at an orgment retreat. Furthermore the leaders, in Lieberman's case, were at least experienced professionals. At the growth centres or the orgment retreats the leaders may lack intelligence, learning or ability of any kind.

Lieberman also studied a control group of 69 students who

wanted to join encounter groups but who could not do so because of conflicts in their schedules. Whereas ten per cent of the participants emerged as casualties none of the controls, who were otherwise attending the same university, showed any such signs or symptoms. This casualty rate, said the researchers, "disturbed us, especially because it probably does not reflect the full extent of damage wrought by the groups." And six months later they still found a ten per cent rate of casualty among the participants.

"Many of the leaders," said Yalom, "were completely unaware that there had been casualties in their groups." The leaders were optimists. They saw some improvement in 90 per cent of group members and high improvement in 30 per cent. The researchers asked the participants to judge themselves on the same scale; they asked co-participants to judge each other, and they checked also for change among significant people in each participant's social network. The enthusiasm of the leaders was not reflected in the ultimate findings of the researchers. Only 14 per cent of the participants had shown high positive change and 20 per cent more had shown some change for the better. After six months both of these figures had dropped still further. On the other end of the scale there were 19 per cent of the participants who were what they called negative changers or outright casualties.

Included in the groups used were two N.T.L. personal growth encounters, an N.T.L. T-group, two different gestalt groups, two psychodrama groups, a psychoanalytically-oriented group, two transactional analysis groups, a Rogerian marathon, a group called Esalen eclectic, an eclectic marathon, a Synanon Game, a T-group, and two Bell and Howell Peer Programs on tape, with no leader. It is intriguing that the type of group bore little or no relation to the production of either casualties or high positive change. What was important was the style of the leader. The most aggressive and stimulating leaders who were, "intrusive, confrontive, challenging" and who revealed a great deal of themselves and were the most charismatic and authoritarian, produced the greatest number of casualties. These men had "a religious aura" about them that caused them to "involve the individual with a system of beliefs and values . . . rather than to encourage the individual to change according to his own needs and potential".

The most vulnerable participants were those who had rather low self-esteem at the beginning of the encounter and a greater expectation that the group would fulfill their needs. Yalom said: "Individuals who are psychologically vulnerable and who over-invest their hopes in the magic of salvation of encounter groups are particularly vulnerable when they interact with leaders who believe they can offer deliverance." Lieberman et al. had themselves been interested in groups for some time and were by no means intent on merely discrediting the movement. Their concern was extremely apparent in their writing, and although they disclosed much evidence that the encounter was indeed a dangerous invention they remained convinced that it could be controlled and rendered useful in the end. They said: "If we no longer expect groups to produce magical, lasting changes and if we stop seeing them as panaceas, we can regard them as useful, socially sanctioned opportunities for human beings to explore and to express themselves. Then we can begin to work on ways to improve them so that they may make a meaningful contribution toward solving human problems."

With all of this I cannot disagree, but it is almost beside the point. The groups that are relevant to the subject of this book are those that Lieberman described as "emotionally stimulating". These are the groups that have been known for many centuries to have a strong and persistent effect on vulnerable or receptive people. The Stanford study, moreover, did not consider the exceedingly important question of organizational development and of the involuntary involvement of people in the techniques of that form. It also did not consider the impact of sensitivity training in grade schools and high schools.

In 1971, Esalen pitched its tents in New York again. This

time John Lilly had returned from Arica and was able to describe the joy of "continuous satori-samadhi". Everything else was the same, and yet something was wrong. Perhaps it was the vibrations. Although many things were done to revive the excitement of 1970, only 2,500 people came to Esalen II, and in 1972 the whole idea of an annual trip to New York was dropped.

Observing the failure of Esalen to arouse attention in New York for more than two consecutive years Bruce Maliver concluded that the fad died in 1971. He said: "The seminar business was slow all over the nation that year. . . ." In short, the encounter movement had peaked, and its rapid decline could now be predicted with some certainty.

A few years ago I noted that the mayfly began its ephemeral life by leaping into the moonlight. It copulated with abandon and died fulfilled within 24 hours. I accordingly proposed that the emblem of the House of Potentialism would most appropriately be the quivering mayfly. No animal in the world lives a more authentic, non-intellectual and tragic life. My relevant and highly innovative suggestion was not picked up by the quivering potentialists, even though a unifying symbol would have greatly advanced their cause.

The American Association of Humanistic Psychology was founded in the early 1960s; in the early 'seventies it is foundering. Its members saw themselves as a third force in that they rejected anti-human behaviourism on the one hand and deterministic psychoanalysis on the other. Of course if the fad really is finished then the most important work, the second phase, must now begin. The believers have not reverted to the positions they held before the miraculous 'sixties when a thousand flowers bloomed. In 1971, Severin Peterson of Stanford documented exultantly that there were 202 different methods of personal growth and these included 10,000 different techniques. In 1967 there were only three growth centres—Esalen and Kairos in California, and Shalal in British Columbia. By late 1971, there were said to be 187 growth centres, most of them in the United

States but 18 in Canada and a few in England, Chile, Germany and Australia. In that year Lee Pulos said: "It has been estimated that one growth centre is being established every two weeks and that one out of three hundred North Americans has taken part in a growth centre programme."

This extraordinary rate of growth has certainly not continued and there is no doubt that the movement has reached its zenith. It would be very unwise for us to conclude, however, that it will now disappear without a trace. The Aureon Institute ran a farm near Woodstock, New York. Its aim was to "uncover and maximize man's inherent resources for living life to the fullest". Its weekends were described by such titles as "The Joy of Play" and "The Quest for Zest". Will this place close its doors? Will its leaders disappear in disillusionment, and its graduates forget everything they learned there? And what about WILL (Workshop Institute for Living and Learning), and GROW (Group Relations Ongoing Workshops), both of New York, the Explorations Institute in Berkeley, and The Centre for the Whole Person in Philadelphia and the Claremont Centre in Toronto? Will absolutely all these organizations and the people associated with them cease and desist? The answer is absolutely in the negative. Many of these centres will close, but most of them will re-adjust their third eye and carry on with the hard work of bringing about the total transformation of our society.

The movement is not dead. It has completed its first ten years of astonishing growth and successfully scattered its ideas across a vast population. It only gives the impression that it is moribund. In fact there are people all across the continent who have yet to be directly affected by the human potential movement and who are as vulnerable today as were the most chic people of the 'sixties. The real work of the humanistic psychologists lies ahead, and this real work will be carried on in respectable disguises designed to allay the apprehensions of the more canny people who are not members of the excitable avant garde of San Francisco and New York.

The claims are still being made, the literature of potentialism is widely available; and the significance of the movement has certainly not been fully determined. Boise and Mobile, unliberated, wait for joy, transcendence, and cultural redefinition. The third five-year plan will attempt to convert the neglected masses waiting in the hinterland, and the casualty rate outside of Stanford will probably exceed ten per cent. We should consider, then, the effects of the movement among many people who may never have heard of Schutz, Perls, Rogers and Bindrim or, for that matter, N.T.L. or Esalen. It is these people who must be changed if the motivational roots of the society are to be profoundly altered.

The Chinese knew that this was so in the years after 1949. The Americans must move inexorably towards the Chinese solution if the ideals of their own great cultural revolution are to be realized. It would seem that every impassioned movement tends to progress from a benign and humanistic philosophy to a doctrinaire and authoritarian reality. And it is at an advanced stage of this process that the casualty rate, whatever it may be, comes to be regarded as tolerable because the cause is great.

The expansion of the movement with fanfare in the 'sixties was intensely interesting, but the quiet insinuation of the movement into every aspect of the society in the 'seventies may turn out to be of far greater importance. It is for this reason that we will require many serious studies into the effects of the group phenomenon. We must learn much more about the casualty rate in diverse circumstances if we desire to protect individual people from injury and if, moreover, we desire to maintain the capacity of our society to defend itself against the influence of those who will continue to insist on radical and irrational change.

8

The Revival of
Magic Humanism

It is *de rigueur* for any defender of the human potential movement to make use of a very simple device to silence his critics. He says: "You are in great company. On June 10, 1969, Congressman Rarick read a wild speech into the *Congressional Record* half as long as a book. It was entitled, 'Sensitivity Training—Network for World Control'." The hapless critic is usually a bit dismayed on learning he is considered at one with those who believe the encounter is a communist plot. He is then assured that Gary Allen has written extensively on this subject in *American Opinion,* journal of the John Birch Society. Now this society is extremist in every sense of the word. Birchers refer constantly to a vast conspiracy that would establish a communist regime in America immediately, but for the fact that there are more guns in the hands of the American people than there are weapons in the rest of the world combined. America is still strong, then, but sensitivity training is weakening it day by day. One has visions of the members of the American Rifle Association staging huge gun burnings in every town square all over the country. It is also pointed out that the Patriotic Letter Writers of Pasadena and the Voice of Americanism in Dallas have shrieked of this communist menace that is specifically designed to brainwash our children, our young people, our clergymen and, believe it or not, even our businessmen.

But why should we care what the John Birch Society says about sensitivity training? The mere fact that this ultraconservative organization has raised its shrill voice against the encounter movement should not intimidate us. Certainly the principle of the kiss of death should not be used to frighten people away from examining every aspect, in as much detail as possible, of what is undoubtedly a major social phenomenon in American life at this time. In *The Encounter Game,* Bruce Maliver addresses himself to this issue. He points out that Carl Rogers has said encounter groups "breed constructive change . . . hence all those who are opposed to change will be stoutly or even violently opposed to the intensive group experience." Maliver observes: "With this simple dismissal of criticism Rogers falls victim to the same reasoning that he attributes to the right winger whom he criticizes, overlooking the possibility that there can be constructive criticism not motivated by political ideology."

Of course Maliver is right; but I would be inclined to ask him what is so wrong with being motivated by a political point of view. There is in our society a very strong tradition of liberal democracy which must certainly be identified as an ideological system. It is characteristically anti-utopian; it emphasizes individual human rights and freedoms; it honours privacy; and it is concerned to let a man be dignified and proud if that is his inclination. The reader will perhaps be able to detect, as I have done, certain tendencies in the human potential movement that are clearly opposed to this liberal democratic tradition. If that is so, and if the further success of the H.P.M. might result in some reduction in the quality of life in our society, then we should not be reluctant to speak freely on this point. We certainly do not need the John Birch Society to define our arguments for us; but we should most emphatically not be dissuaded by the facile

allegation that the Birchers are people whose political per-
suasions are similar to ours.

The term "alternate society" is really a poor one because
diversity has been one of the most noticeable characteristics of
our society for centuries. Indeed the Counter Culture, as one of
these alternatives, is by no means a new phenomenon. However
in recent years a very concerted attempt has been made to
isolate and describe a particular ideological position that is
sharply at variance with that of the complex inclusive society.
This Counter Culture has itself taken two rather distinct forms
although these are related. The one is activist and militant, the
other pacifist. Both are convinced that the general society is
something no enlightened person should be associated with. The
first group would change it by promoting revolution; the second
would drop out and attempt to survive either self-reliantly or
parasitically, usually in a communal setting.

The philosophic position characteristic of the Counter Culture
in both its forms is often called radical humanism by its
adherents, but I prefer the term "magic humanism". This system
of ideas has a very long history, but we may begin by examining
it in one of its modern and most fashionable forms. My illustration will serve also to emphasize that radical humanism has
penetrated quite deeply into the fabric of our culture.

Among the most respectable of the growth centres that have
come to my attention is the one at Atikokan, Ontario. The
Quetico Centre has a president and a large board of directors.
It has a group of distinguished advisers and a further group of
even more celebrated patrons. One of these was the late Rt. Hon.
Lester B. Pearson.

On the letterhead of the centre there is an inscription that
reads: "A residential continuing education centre engaged in
shaping the future. It is committed to the belief that a prime
motivation of social growth and change is man's need to fulfil
his potential." Now I think it would be useful for us to determine
what would be the shape of the future if it were designed accord-

ing to the model proposed by the Quetico Centre. Fortunately I have in my possession a most revealing little paper, published by the Quetico Centre, that may help us to discern a number of the characteristics of that ideal model. I would like to examine this paper, *Transition,* in some detail because, though it is brief, it manages to touch on virtually every value honoured by the Counter Culture today. Yet this is not a publication of the underground press. It is a publication of the Quetico Centre of Atikokan, Ontario. People from many great corporations and branches of government travel to this centre to attend managerial grid seminars. Organization development is one of the primary interests of the Quetico Centre. Its director is in some demand as a consultant to organizations which, in their desire to be fashionable, have decided to institute O.D.

The inscription heading page one of *Transition* differs interestingly from the one I have already quoted from the letterhead. This one is much less confusing, and reads ". . . dedicated to the belief that social change, to be effective, must affect the motivational roots of a society." *Transition* itself begins by offering an exceedingly transparent little test designed, it notes, to help the reader examine the assumptions and values underlying his way of life. This test, headed "Who am I"? is composed of 16 statements, and the reader is asked to determine to what extent he agrees with each of them. Two scores result from this exercise. The W score indicates to what extent one's values are of the "old culture"; the Z score indicates one's attachment to the "new culture". It may please the curious reader to know that I scored disastrously badly on that part of the test that indicated subscription to those cultural factors identified by the centre as showing approval of the new culture.

Now this little test was almost entirely based on an article written by Philip E. Slater called "Cultures in Collision". In this article Slater savagely attacked what he described as the "Old Culture", and offered in its place the beautiful "New Culture" of the young and the liberated. The Quetico Centre apparently swallowed the whole thing and rejoiced in this further support of its pre-conceived ideas on the need for radical change in our society. After all, Slater had said: "A cultural system is a dynamic whole, resting on processes that must be accelerative to be self-sustaining. Change must therefore affect the motivational roots of a society or it is not change at all". In surveying the battleground, Slater concluded: "There is no such thing as compromise."

It might be instructive to consider a few of the statements set forth in the test prepared by the Quetico Centre. One of them is: "Important material needs are easily satisfied and the resources for doing so are plentiful." Now to qualify as a member of the new enlightenment one must strongly agree with this statement. According to Philip Slater, "almost everything is at issue in the war between the young and their elders." The elders, the paper explains, "live in a culture (old) based on the concept of scarcity; everything rests on the assumption that the world does not contain the wherewithal to satisfy the needs of its human inhabitants." This is a shattering statement. According to this view, the Pope is a raging member of the New Culture. There is enough for everyone at the banquet of life, as he puts it, and it is therefore immoral to make any attempt to check the explosive increase in the population of the world. Members of the old culture are afraid, but the Quetico Centre is not afraid, because scarcity is an illusion.

Again, "The biblical directive, 'Work, for the night is coming,' is as essential in the 1970s as it was in biblical times." To be a member of the old culture one would have to be strongly in agreement with this statement. A poet of my acquaintance observed it was a wonderful thing that the new culture had solved the ancient problem of physical survival. The night would no longer come. At long last, the grasshopper is vindicated and the ant stands revealed as a pathetic fool. I am reminded of a radio interview I heard recently. A very liberated member of the movement who held that it was the hated Protestant ethic that drove people to work was asked by the interviewer about, for example, the night shift at the general hospital. The answer was surpassingly arrogant: "There will always be enough stupid nurses who will be willing to work all night long." At any rate the Quetico Centre strongly admires the free and creative person whose Z score is very high. Such a person will condemn this ancient directive, whatever its meaning may be. The person whose W score is high will wonder who, finally, will keep things going while all the spontaneous and evolved people are living urgently in the present, fulfilling themselves, and learning about the revolution.

Again, "Competition is unnecessary and the only danger to humans is human aggression." This is an especially interesting statement. To be a member of the new culture one must strongly agree with it. Competition, it is imagined, is a detestable invention of western capitalism. The new culture replaces competition with co-operation. In any case two statements are contained in this item, and one could easily answer these differently. Competition might, for example, seem unnecessary in many situations, but quite a large number of elemental hazards surround man other than his angry and irrational fellows. That man is dangerous is not at issue. It is the image of all the happy trainers at the Quetico Centre, drawing the attention of their trainees eagerly to the pronouncement of this new authority, that is most annoying to me. Yes, human aggression is a threat to every one of us, but in spite of its espousal of love and peace, the new culture is not quite free of it. Recently I saw a merry description on the jacket of a youth walking peacefully down the street. In rather large letters it read: "If you are not ready to kill your parents you are not ready for the revolution." This statement was commonly heard in the countries of eastern Europe before 1917. Similarly I saw a letter written from one person to another that concluded "Peace, Love, State of War". Only a very ignorant person could strongly agree with both parts of the statement about competition and the aggressiveness of man.

Again: "To accumulate possessions is to deliver pieces of one's self to dead things." In the new culture all dead things are to be collectively owned. Private ownership is anathema. It is as simple as that. The new culture, says Slater, "argues that instead of throwing away one's body so that one can accumulate material artifacts one should throw away the artifacts and enjoy one's body". In the new culture personal relating counts for everything. But this is the essential dictum of the human potential movement and that is why I consider it useful to discuss Slater in such detail. The business organization or branch of government that sends its people to the Quetico Centre is sending them to a place that makes every effort to instil in them a belief in the values of the Counter Culture. These values may be regarded as good or bad; but that they are strongly taught as good in the human growth centres cannot be denied. I happen to think that it is potentially destructive to society and, in many cases, to the individual people subjected to indoctrination. The T-group and the other techniques used at such centres are not, after all, lacking in potency.

"Communal love is more important than parental love," Quetico tells us. The consequences flowing from the notion that brotherhood transcends all other kinds of love are known to everyone except, of course, the magic humanists. I will return to this point but for the moment I will only remind the reader that all the excitement at the centre derives from the messianic urge to implement the principles of humanistic management. The trainee knows very well that if he is to be approved of he must strongly agree that communal love is supreme. If he fails to agree to this he is a member of the old culture and as such he is in need of considerably more training.

Finally: "Being consistently authentic, whole, real in one's business and private life is essential to mental health." I have included this test item not because it can be literally understood but because it contains the key word "authentic." It is one of the fondest wishes of the human potential movement that everyone shall be authentic in all things. Now to be authentic, for these people, implies a willingness to express spontaneously what one feels at any given moment and in any place. He who would choose to withhold such feelings is not authentic. He may breathe and occupy a certain space but he is not authentic. However by far the most sinister aspect of this particular value is that which is expressed at the end of the Quetico Centre's statement. He who is not authentic cannot be mentally well. This should elevate the seriousness of this discussion by several orders of magnitude. The person who resists emotional incontinence is sick. He who is sick is in need of treatment. Treatment involves the exhibition of a variety of techniques designed to bring about mental health. In the case of the human potential movement the sickness of a person who is not authentic is cured through his participation in the T-group or one of its successors.

In the Counter Culture it is held that the ideal society is one in which complete openness is the rule. This means, of course, that no secrets concerning any subject whatsoever may be withheld from anyone. The society, moreover, is to be communal. That is to say love for one's parents, children or other relatives is especially condemned. It is love for the members of the group and, by extension, for all mankind that is to be honoured. The old culture, it is said, is especially inclined to be violent. The new culture, solving once again this ancient problem through the mechanism of simple denial, rejects violence and celebrates sexuality instead. It would seem that sexuality and violence are mutually exclusive. The old culture, hateful, frightened, striving and aggressive, stresses competition and the survival of the fittest. The new culture stresses gratification of the senses, co-operation and self-actualization in the immediate and glittering present.

The Counter Culture is especially concerned to condemn private property. All personal objects will be owned by the community. All thoughts, ideas and feelings will also be shared by the entire population. In the new society there will be neither private possessions nor privacy. In fact there will be no individuality. This is put most succinctly by Philip Slater in his article: "Nothing will change until individualism is assigned a subordinate place in the American value system—for individualism lies at the core of the old culture . . . ."

The new Counter Culture, notes *Transition,* reverses all priorities of the old culture. The Counter Culture is based on the assumption that important human needs are easily satisfied, and that the resources for doing so are plentiful. *Transition* continues, quoting Slater really: "There is no reason outside of human perversity for peace not to reign and for life not to be spent in the cultivation of joy and beauty. Those who can do this in the face of the old culture's ubiquity are considered beautiful." The magic humanists turn their third eye to the tumultuous world, and seeing nothing, speak of joy and beauty everlasting.

The reader may now be interested to know how well I scored on that part of the test that was said to measure one's affinity for the old culture. The answer is that I scored almost as low a mark as I did on the new culture section. My overall score, accordingly, was dismally low. According to the Quetico Centre a person whose overall score is very low may live an impoverished life, on this account, because he tends to shy away from basic value judgments. It would seem that in my condition I cannot be a supporter of culture in any form. I am neither young nor old, fossilized nor free. I stand neither at the pole sanctified by the Quetico Centre nor at the pole identified by the editors of this centre as representing that of the Establishment. This is an interesting point. The person who is wholeheartedly able to subscribe to the values of the new culture is an exemplary person. He is even beautiful. Yet the only way one can score a high mark on the new culture scale is to agree strongly with certain obvious statements and never mildly agree or disagree with any of them. The idol of the new culture, therefore, is an extremist. Furthermore the most dangerous adversary of the movement is not by any means the man who is such a caricature of the 19th-century tycoon that he scores furiously and with clenched fists in favour of all the negative statements. The person who is most dangerous to the movement is he who refuses to take either of these extreme positions. But this person, according to the centre, lives an impoverished life because he is afraid to express a strong opinion. He is particularly in need of treatment, I should think; but he will be a difficult case. The extreme radicals of the right can be converted into extreme radicals of the left without much difficulty. They are not so far apart to begin with because the spectrum from right to left describes a curve the tips of which finally overlap. It is the person whose values range within these two extremes, who appreciates his own intellect, and who is appalled by spectacles in which the rationality of other men is suspended, that represents the final enemy of the extremists. He is, I am pleased to say, a worthy adversary. And this is one of the reasons why not every radical movement has completed the course of its natural history from provocative tract to savage aggression.

But now, what about this one small excrescence of the Counter Culture that I have used by way of illustration? Is the editor of *Transition* completely atypical of the staff of the Quetico Centre? Do the other staff members, including the director, subscribe to the value system of the editor? It is a matter of the greatest importance that the supervisor referred to in the chapter on orgment be told precisely what will be the real—authentic, if you like—values of his trainers. He may not desire to be rendered suggestible and subscribe to the values of the Counter Culture. And even if he should prove resistant to training he might not desire to be subjected to the concerted efforts of the staff, and the other members of his group, to improve his mental health, for six consecutive days. It is not agreeable to be intractable within a small and concentrated society of believers all of whom are intensely concerned to destroy your resistance so that you may experience the joy of self-realization. It might be worse than merely disagreeable. It might be, to an informed and intelligent person, an indication that such vital concepts as freedom and individuality were being attacked once again. He might feel moreover that the projection of this tendency into the future might bring about a social condition that would be seriously threatening to the society.

Philip Slater reveals a curious bit of knowledge. He says: "Every revolution is in part a revival." He is quite right, of course, but it is unusual for a prophet of any age to recognize that his work is a variety of reincarnation. In the 1830s, for example, there was an intriguing movement in the United States known as Transcendentalism; the main contributors to this reaction against the prevailing social norms were Henry David Thoreau and Ralph Waldo Emerson. These men, the poet Walt Whitman, and still later, R. M. Bucke, the author of the strange and irrational book *Cosmic Consciousness,* all came to realize that industrial and urban society was profoundly hurtful to man and they retreated, accordingly, into the uncompromising but somehow far more satisfying arms of nature. In the wilderness they found moral and spiritual gratification; they found themselves by transcending the rational conservatism of their time. Their society was, of course, undergoing rapid change due to the inexorable advance of industrialism. The old order had already been violently smashed in France; but the new order, humane and enlightened, had soon been converted by St. Just, Robespierre and many others into dogma, terror and finally military conquest. The Transcendentalists lived in the time of the first general wars and the rise of international capitalism. They saw that man was being engulfed by the horrors of economic and political control and they developed accordingly a radical solution that was centred on the individual but which involved his withdrawal into a spiritual communion with his fellows and with the natural world.

Almost 150 years later Philip Slater points out that rugged individualism and the antique concept of the nuclear family are the cause of the old culture's fascination with scarcity. Moreover it is scarcity that brings on sexual repression, competitiveness and a guiding belief in inequality. The horrors consequent upon this conviction that scarcity is imminent are many, according to Slater. In fact the whole of American civilization can be explained on the basis of this incredibly simplistic notion. Slater seems to regret that his solution would resemble any well-developed totalitarian state. In fact his reduction of individuality, and his emphasis on cooperation and communal life with a complete absence of competition would result, if such a plan were implemented, in a social system very similar to that which may now be found in China. Even so Slater concludes that this is the only way to dispel the alienation and loneliness that are now, he claims, characteristic of our society.

In our own time, then, we may observe the emergence of a new transcendentalism and this movement, like the first, is fundamentally a reaction against what is perceived to be an authoritarian and inhibiting society. Of the greatest significance, however, is that whereas the romantic thinkers of the 19th Century were few in number and by no means capable of influencing the general society in any profound way, the new romantics of the 20th Century have been able to make use of a vast communications network for the transmission of their ideas. Once again the message has been that man's society is corrupt and corrupting, but there has been one extremely different element in the neo-transcendentalist programme: the group, and not the individual, is to bring about renewal and salvation.

The problems of society are, of course, no less complicated than they were in the 1830s. The great institutions are even more powerful and controlling and man has had to adapt to an astonishing series of scientific and bureaucratic threats to his dignity and freedom. Many people have commented on this; but the most influential of the philosophes of the American enlightenment have probably been Herbert Marcuse and Norman O. Brown. Douglas McGregor's influence has been very great, of course, but his name is by no means as familiar as are those of the others. At the basis of the criticism of these men has been the belief that life in the modern industrial state has become progressively more cold and limited. In this deplorable circumstance, the human being longs for release, but he is caught between an impersonal educational system and a vicious and competitive vocational one. Science has debunked the religions of the past and the technocratic state has fragmented society and pressed man mercilessly against the very machines he himself created. Human feeling has particularly been suppressed, and with that an ancient human longing for unity with all men and nature has arisen. Once again, transcendence has seemed utterly necessary, and as always this has implied a revival of mysticism, of the cult of the irrational, the immediate and the spontaneous.

Norman O. Brown felt that repression must be utterly abolished and that there should be no restraints on behaviour. The super ego was the forbidding conscience of man and as such it was harmful to him and to the realization of his fullest potential. In *Love's Body,* Brown wrote: "The real world is the world where thoughts are omnipotent, where no distinction is drawn between wish and deed." He said further that it is necessary "to find the kingdom in one's own body, and to find one's own body in the outside world. The body to be realized is the body of the cosmic man, the body of the universe is one perfect man."

It is not difficult to see why Brown's obscurity and mysticism would be very appealing to the neotranscendentalists of our time. He proposes an ill-defined religiousness with his references to the cosmos and the unity of all men and nature, but in the end his work amounts to a species of mindless religiosity.

There have been, of course, a number of other contributors to the theory and practice of magic humanism. Theodore Roszak refers to the super consciousness that is appearing in the Counter Culture and that overflows all logic and limit. Charles Reich, briefly the most fashionable spokesman for the counter culture, refers to Consciousness III.

Several years ago J. K. Galbraith noted in *the New Industrial State* that the technocrat, a new kind of man, had risen to a position of great power in our society. Reich points out, accordingly, that the "corporate state" is a monstrous thing that developed on the basis of what he calls "Consciousness I thinking". Presumably this condition of the mind is what is referred to by Slater as the old culture. However this industrial monolith is actually controlled by people who think on the level of what Reich calls Consciousness II. This, I suppose, is the corporate liberalism of the sort that began with the New Deal and which has developed in a progressively more socialist way from the 'thirties to the present time. Reich concludes that this arrangement has resulted in institutions that are inimical to man's freedom and happiness. Everything, education, politics, the law, the economic system, is designed to perpetuate this grotesque and fundamentally anti-human system. But only the children, and Reich, and the other social critics whom I have already mentioned, know that this is so. And these enlightened people have now appeared on the scene with the Answer. The Answer is Consciousness III. Naturally the Consciousness III person is receptive to immediate experience and he is interested in a system of values that is altogether non-material. He is, above all, authentic. This term is always used in such a way as to deny legitimacy to everyone who fails to see that total and naive openness in every situation is always desirable. Anyone who opposes an ideal system is by definition lacking in virtue and enlightenment. The value of the Counter Culture is simply self-evident. It is unthinkable that it will not, in time, prevail.

Reich's book became a best seller, but his three levels of consciousness were just as vividly described about eight hundred years ago. I refer to the vision of Joachim of Fiore, who lived from 1145 to 1202. This Calabrian hermit became convinced on the basis of his intensive study of the Bible that history must be perceived as an ascent through three successive ages. The first age was that of the father or the law, and its sacred book the Old Testament. The second age was that of the son, and its sacred work the New Testament. The third age was that of the spirit. In the first age men were afraid and the world was lit by starlight. In the second age, the dawn, men discovered faith and filial piety. The third age, according to the prophecies of Joachim, would be one in which love and freedom would prevail and the joy of the Holy Ghost would illuminate the hearts of all men. The world would become one vast monastery, a new Eden; and this state would last for a thousand years until the moment of the last judgment.

There is, it need hardly be necessary to point out, a direct line of descent from Joachim of Fiore to the theories of John of Leyden and the Anabaptists, the philosophes of the French enlightenment, the German idealist philosophers Lessing and Schelling, and the utopians of Brook Farm. Indeed the Marxist ideals of equality and fraternity and the ultimate withering away of the state are descended from this idea and so, too, is the curious fantasy of Charles Reich who predicts the necessary reduction of the two old cultures and their replacement with the fabulous condition known as the Third Consciousness. The breathless anticipation of the Age of Aquarius, or whatever else it may be called, is certainly an indication of the rebirth in our time of an ancient myth, but we must be aware of the fact that this myth is an expression of one of the most profound needs of man: the need to give birth to *Homo transcendentia* with his rule of peace and bliss. And the onset of the millennium is always considered to be imminent. That is one of its most persistent characteristics. The time to be saved is always now because the end is always threateningly near.

But there is a far greater problem here. Such utopian formulations as the one proposed by Reich tend to be self-fulfilling prophesies. If alienation and discontent are observed in a large population then the solution, presumably, is to draw it to the attention of everyone that alienation and discontent exist and that civil disobedience in the face of repressive laws is absolutely indicated. This was certainly the position of Marcuse, and in so speaking he may initially have entranced a great many youthful dissidents, but he also greatly alarmed all those learned, intelligent and socially conscious people who were actually trying to right some of the wrongs of the society. A divisive trend, once begun, can be controlled for a while by expressions of interest in self-fulfillment and harmony, but in the course of time the maintenance of this pretence becomes a burden. When sincerity and openness are cardinal virtues, as they often are in radical movements, the maintenance of this pretence becomes impossible. In the natural history of such movements the mask of moderation is always thrown down and the actual position of the leader and his straggling flock is revealed as being in closer proximity to the pole than anyone had imagined.

Recruits to any new movement have been drawn, at various times, from nearly every part of society; but there is absolutely no doubt that today by far the most productive field is that of the affluent middle class. It is especially in this group that one may find those people who most intensely desire to become enlightened and socially aware in the shortest possible time. It is in this group today—as it was in the Weimar Republic in the 'twenties—that one may find people who are most receptive to the notion that man, if he is to fulfil his destiny on earth, must be freed from the chains of his conserved culture. These are the people most urgently driven toward a vision of the millennium, and they are very often as sincere as they are misguided.

These are the people who are the natural prey of the extremists. They are not raging revolutionaries themselves, in the beginning, but, in the course of time, their activities tend to complement the work of those who are more consciously engaged in the systematic destruction of the society. They are always disillusioned in the end of course, but until the day of their real enlightenment they remain true believers in the virtues of the new culture. The harsh and heartless people who are alarmed at the prospect of radical change are the representatives of the old culture.

It is always the same. In every age the radical reformers are quite sure that all of the ills of the world are referable to the fossilized conservatism of the people who maintain the established culture. It is these reactionaries who must be discredited along with the values of the institutions they uphold. And all this must be done in the interests of the people. The reformers always know what is best for the people. Finally, of course, social upheaval and supreme sacrifice must be endured by everyone, but by that time the reformers have been removed from the scene, or have themselves become conservative, and the primal need to survive justifies any action. The early period in which the mask was naively worn becomes an anguished memory.

"This is the task of our century, to create a new human type out of a new life myth." The magic humanists are perfectly comfortable with this statement, of course, but they do not know who wrote it. Even so they would be inclined to applaud so relevant a statement until they heard that it was made by Alfred Rosenberg, the approved philosopher of the National Socialist Party.

"The status quo is intolerable. An establishment is stifling all progress. The spontaneous anger of all the young forces of the nation must rise up and smash the old system and release all the pent up forces of renewal and revolution." This statement would certainly be one that the radical humanists would admire. Some of them might wish that they had been clever enough to compose such a necessary exhortation to social change themselves. Unfortunately it was uttered fifty years ago in a country that was being prepared for cataclysmic change. But then Benito Mussolini was a fascist, and so he was probably only trying to stir up a lot of trouble for no good purpose.

Since the Second World War we have been addressed by a whole series of new prophets who have tried to increase our awareness of the iniquity of the establishment that is stifling all progress. In fact these people have managed to bring into being an utopian literature as persuasive as was the astoundingly similar literature produced in the 18th Century by Rousseau, Morelly, Helvétius, Mably, and many others. With respect to the ultimately disastrous results of the work of the philosophes Talmon points out that there is an absolute incompatibility between an all-solving creed and liberty. These two ideals are profoundly important to man but whenever he attempts to satisfy both of them simultaneously the result is hypocrisy, self deception and oppression. Talmon says: "This is the curse on salvationist creeds: to be born of the noblest impulses of man and to degenerate into weapons of tyranny." The reason for this is that a creed that is perfect by definition cannot tolerate opposition. And the collective will of the group, as soon as it is institutionalized, becomes an essential aspect of such a perfect creed. Freedom has absolutely no meaning if in a social situation the right to differ is denied.

Our own philosophes, undeterred by such historical arguments, continued to define the nature of the utopian state—very nearly, of the natural order; and during the 'sixties the revolt that was seen as inevitable by the earlier thinkers actually came into being with the creation of a fairly identifiable Counter Culture. Theodore Roszak in *The Making of a Counter Culture* held that society was something to which no sane man could possibly adapt. The Counter Culture, on the other hand, offered the only hope of preserving man's embattled humanity. Power would be decentralized against the dread trend, and every enlightened man would be entirely open to the idea of communal living and to the easy acceptance of eroticism and the non-rational aspects of living in the world. Roszak was clearly impressed with everything that seemed visionary. He was, accordingly, very taken with William Blake and also with such oriental religious systems as Zen Buddhism and Hinduism. Most importantly Roszak proposed that man must be subjective. To be objective was to impose an intellectual restraint on one's imagination and this was an operation that was altogether artificial and inhuman.

In fact one cannot entirely disagree with this view. Rationality does not come most easily to man; it is clearly the most recently developed of all his faculties and in all his phylogenic history it is the one characteristic that most clearly separates him from the beasts. Man can actually think, review the past and plan certain actions that will tend to improve his chances of survival in the future. It is rather easier for man to be irrational and magical because such activities are more primitive and they set aside those parts of the brain that are of most recent origin. Nevertheless it would not be wise for us to conclude that because irrationality is natural to man this must be his essential mode or, particularly, that it must be his best. If birds evolved wings after many centuries but retained the capacity to walk it would not be correct to assume that the most natural activity of birds is walking. It would be better to say that birds fly and that this is their supreme achievement but that they can also walk, and this is something of the greatest importance to them as well. Man can make use of a unique intellect but he can also be irrational. For the new philosophes, however, it is his capacity to be irrational that is most pleasing, and everything that demands intellectual activity is condemned as being unnatural and hateful. In short the concept of the noble savage has been revived in our time and this concept is as foolish and limiting as it was when it first became fashionable in 18th-century France. For Roszak and the others it is feeling that is of paramount importance: thinking is basically dangerous. Objectivity and the scientific method reduce man and jam him into a steel cage.

Roszak seemed to turn some of the ideas of Hegel and Marx inside out. Whereas the creators of communist ideology seemed to feel that if the social environment could be changed then man would automatically change for the better, Roszak et al. seemed to feel that a new consciousness would bring about change in political and social institutions. And the instruments that would be most effective in creating this new consciousness were the illusionogenic drugs and the encounter group both of which specifically reduce a man's capacity to think. Under the influence of his shaman and a potent drug Carlos Casteneda said: "For the first time in my life I felt the encumbering weight of my reason. An indescribable anguish overtook me." This horror of reason, which is clearly an aspect of the new culture, causes those of us who are not agonized by consciousness to react most negatively. The communal impulse also arouses much suspicion among those who appreciate individuality and privacy.

In fact all of our new extremists have promoted a deepening distrust of the institutions of social control that are essential for the maintenance of the stability and security of the majority of people. The conservatives, and the liberals too for that matter, are interested in maintaining the essential outlines of our society as it gradually evolves and improves. Thoughtful men do not desire violent revolutions or any of the disruptions that lead inexorably toward that appalling social condition. Yet a literal interpretation of the work of most of these prophets could easily cause suggestible and inexperienced people to conclude that revolution was not only unavoidable but altogether necessary. It is the intense anti-intellectualism of the Counter Culture that is so potentially threatening to this society. In such groups there is a vastly increased tendency to subscribe uncritically to the values of whatever ideological system is offered by the charismatic leader of the day. In 1425, it was the children of Florence whom Savanarola was able to recruit into his monstrous antisocial assault. In the 'thirties the Hitler Youth was an irresistible force in the maintainance of the Nazi power. In the 'sixties the Red Guards of China were among the most fanatical of the people in the search and destroy missions against those wretched people who still maintained any sort of appreciation of the past.

Our own new culture is exceedingly retrogressive. It proposes as its paradigm a primitive egalitarian society in which all men are equal in every sense—and not just before the law. Such a condition only appears in primitive hunting and gathering bands. As soon as agriculture in its simplest form begins to appear such communities begin to differentiate among the diverse human resources of the population. The Counter Culture, however, would not just return to the forests to establish a beautiful communal group. It would create a community that was basically unserious and dependent on the persistence of a supportive larger society. It would create a society, moreover, that was based on a sort of easy mysticism; and this is why the illusionogenic drugs have been largely accepted by its adherents. Gratification must not be postponed and it must be as intense as possible. Such gratification is seen as occurring most excellently in the course of an altered state of consciousness.

The urge for satisfaction has thus taken a very shallow form in today's Counter Culture. The ethical position that has usually been associated with religious systems in the past has here been reduced to a belief in the virtues of non-self-denial. The supplicant to this particular altar, moreover, thinks neither of his past nor of his future. The gratification is limited to the experience of the high feeling in the immediate present; and as soon as it is over the seeker after experience must begin his search again just as though nothing had happened to him at all. For this reason he will move constantly in a more radical direction until only the extremes of experience will be satisfying to him. To promote a system of belief that has at its centre such an impoverished state of the mind is to do injustice to the dignity of man.

The magic humanists tend, in my view, to be well meaning but misguided and naive. They talk interminably about relevance, openness and self-realization, but to the extent that they are successful in recruiting people to the armies of the new reformation they diminish man and reduce the quality of his society. In the next chapter I will consider the impact of the values of the magic humanist in diverse places. One of these is education, a field that has been a special target in recent years and which, as a result, has experienced particular agony. In responding to the relentless attack on language which has been one of the essential characteristics of the H.P.M. Brian Meeson said: "Any move to reduce the centrality of the discipline of language within a society is to be regarded as a major cultural and political shift. To make it a voluntary pursuit is a form of regressive taxation, in that it may remove from a young person the right to an as-yet-undeveloped property. Language is his birthright. Devaluation of this major human resource is a reduction of democratic rights. A citizenry less skilled in the exercise of precise language is easier wooed by the numbing saturation of political doubletalk."

The new culture is intensely suspicious of language because it is the basic instrument of the intellect. The new culture begins by declaring that freedom is exhibited only when feelings are unrestrainedly expressed. It proceeds from this premise to conclude that the precise and subtle use of language is a hindrance to the only sort of expression that really matters; and therefore it promotes the abandonment of both art and discipline. The proponents of the new culture seem to be entirely unable to understand that this process leads inexorably towards the creation of the reductive language that George Orwell called Newspeak. "Oldspeakers unbellyfeel Engsoc" or, members of the old culture who speak the English of the past are quite unable to feel in their very guts the absolute perfection of Big Brother and the principles of The Party. It is distressing that those who today consider themselves to be the most progressive members of our society are convinced that language is the enemy of freedom. It is appalling that such people are so strongly represented in education and the social sciences, fields that are critically important in maintaining or altering the motivational roots, as they put it, of society.

9

School Games
and Party Games

Swift was such a cynical and devious man. He mocked the
illustrious thinkers and professors of his day by describing their
ideas and projects as though they were preposterous. For example he had Gulliver visit the Grand Academy of Lagado
where, to his astonishment, he saw great men engaged in many
brilliant projects all designed to improve the quality of the
civilization of that country. In the School of Languages Gulliver
was impressed by a project "to shorten discourse by cutting
polysyllables into one, and leaving out verbs and participles,
because in reality all things imaginable are but nouns".

The second project Gulliver saw was even more progressive.
This "was a scheme for entirely abolishing all words whatsoever;
and this was urged as a great advantage in point of health as
well as brevity. For it is claimed, that every word we speak is
in some degree a diminution of our lungs by corrosion, and
consequently contributes to the shortening of our lives".

The thinkers of Lagado were very wise in urging the abolition
of language, but having achieved this position they gave up their

advantage by concluding that the people should carry with them all manner of things which they would show to one another in order to converse. Swift, and the thinkers of Lagado, failed entirely to see that to reduce the language to nouns, and substitute nouns with things, did not really mean any escape at all from the burden of intellectual communication. This plan was absurd and impractical.

The answer that eluded Swift has now been found. Communication must be non-verbal if it is to be authentic. In 1973 the Faculty of Education at York University in Toronto began developing a "Teacher Education Curriculum" that would prepare people for work in the classrooms of the future. Naturally enough, English does not appear as a subject in this curriculum. There is, however, something called "The Communication Arts Programme" that sounds as though it might be a descendant of that antique discipline. The director writes: "Human beings communicate in many ways. Schools conventionally have stressed verbal modes and have concentrated on teaching reading and writing." The teacher of the future, the director points out, should be "able to help children to learn to communicate in different ways and to move comfortably from one mode to another."

The objective of the Teacher Education Programme, then, is to "very consciously design a set of experiences for our students which counter the socialization forces present in many schools, which break down their stereotype of teacher role and teacher behaviour, and which help them to acquire the skills, knowledge, and disposition necessary to operate in the emerging schools." The reader will hardly have to be told the small-group seminar will be the essential instrument for "socializing our students toward change".

The ideas of the H.P.M. have been enormously influential in education and there is no indication that this aspect of its work has reached the peak referred to in Chapter Seven. The "new teachers" are being created at a number of education colleges, while the "old teachers" are subjected to retraining at orgment retreats.

The York County Board of Education, for example, has established an organizational development unit. It is the responsibility of this unit to reorient the 120 school administrators, 2,500 teachers and, finally, the 100,000 students in its district. As always, training begins at the top and gradually works downward in the typical pyramid to involve the people on the line. In this case the county retained Dr. Robert B. Morton of Sacramento, California as its consultant. Morton has said: "The Organization Training Laboratory attempts to change not only the individual but the organizational climate in which the individual must continue to work."

Setting up his laboratory at a local motel, Morton began running one-week sessions at which participants "dialogued" and "critiqued" in leaderless groups. The administrators were the first to go. It was a typical orgment affair, and the county was soon deeply involved, even though it had not been adequately established that such a programme was useful or that it was entirely free of risk. It would appear also that the county's teachers, taxpayers and parents were not consulted before this elaborate and expensive programme was undertaken. There is seldom anything democratic about the institution of an orgment plan, whether it occurs in a government agency or in a school system. It was the trendy thing to do, regardless of the cost in dollars and human stress. Max Birnbaum had written: "During the 1960s public education discovered the emotions. Cognitive learning and skill training, the traditional components of education, no longer satisfied. . . . The result was a growing interest in various approaches to affective learning that assigned to the emotional factor in education a role as important as—or, perhaps, more important than—the traditional substantive content and skills. Among these approaches the most enthusiastically embraced has been the so-called sensitivity training."

Birnbaum said that sensitivity training held "tremendous

potential for . . . helping teachers to learn how to use the classroom group for learning purposes". Now that is the real point of this discussion. The teacher who attends an orgment seminar may or may not be impressed by his experience, but he will not fail to observe that his board has approved of the techniques and ideas of the movement and will eventually conclude that it is his further duty to teach his students what he himself has learned about the advantages of non-cognitive learning. As a result we have had T-groups and encounters in classrooms all across the continent, with teachers playing the role of trainers. At the orgment centres the trainers may be experienced and learned in the social sciences, but the teacher, exposed for a week on four different occasions as in the York County case, is not thereby qualified as an encounter leader. His pupils have not been properly screened; they may be unaware of their right to withdraw from the encounter; they are not, therefore, protected from the possibility of psychological and physical injury; and most frequently their parents are entirely ignorant of the fact that this process is going on.

An interesting though rather minor example of this sort of thing was described to me by one of my own children who attends a high school which has not been particularly involved in the rage for sensitivity. In the history class a pattern was presented to the students which, to my readers, will be immediately recognizable as a derivative of the famous Blake Grid. It was, however, a test of the quality of every child's mother. This grid was composed of 100 squares and thus there were ten points running up the left hand and ten running along the base. This large square was then divided into four quarters. On the left was the label, "CONSIDERATION", and below the square was the label, "TASK". The lower left-hand quarter was marked "OVERWHELMED". A mother who scored in this position lacked both consideration and an interest in the work of the house. The upper left-hand quarter was marked "SMOTHER-MOTHER", obviously representing the overprotective parent.

The lower right quarter was marked "ZOO KEEPER", a term that is self-explanatory. The upper right quarter, corresponding to Blake's 9,9 manager, was marked "SUPER MOTHER". The children were invited to judge their mothers in this history class according to a number of criteria, and plot the results on the grid. The significance of the exercise is that it was clearly an intrusion on the part of the teacher into certain highly personal aspects of the children's lives. It was not particularly comfortable for some of the children to have to report that their mothers were "zoo keepers", or that they were defective in some other way. It was all so unnecessary, and so very much removed from the legitimate work of the high school.

Jane Howard cites the case of an English teacher at the Evanston Township High School who was convinced that personal growth was a "more important objective of English classes than literature". She points out that "many of his students and their parents were enthusiastic about the non-verbal exercises he conducted and found them quite valuable." If my child had been studying English with this particular teacher I would not have been among those parents who found his exercises commendable or, as it is put in the H.P.M. "relevant".

In fact there was controversy all across the continent concerning "affective education" and its essential anti-intellectualism. Nevertheless the trend continued. Sensitivity training was conducted at every level from the first grade to graduate courses in social work. An excellent illustration of this trend occurred at the Psychiatric Institute of the University of Maryland. Sensitivity training laboratories conducted in a residential setting 35 miles from Baltimore were attended by psychiatric residents, their wives, and a number of nurses. The institute also sent its psychiatric residents and nurses to sensitivity training laboratories run by the N.T.L. at Bethel. Many such programmes made attendance at the laboratories a course requirement. In such cases it would not be possible for a student to decline the invitation to travel to the orgment retreat or refuse to participate in its activities.

Reading *Joy,* the thrillingly optimistic book by Will Schutz, I was seriously shocked when I got to page 222. Up to that point Schutz had described his work as a "behaviour-science consultant" to several schools on both coasts. He had described various encounter groups involving superintendents, teachers, parents and students. Harmony and open and honest exchange had always been the result. He was particularly pleased with the work of a Grade 12 teacher who conducted 15 three-hour encounter sessions and brought about, in the children, a greater awareness of their own needs and a much less conformist attitude. Finally, Schutz said: "I am more convinced than ever that we are on the right track in the attempt to have students deal with their feelings in the class, as well as the content of the subject." I was only surprised when he referred to this nasty business of the content; I was overwhelmed, therefore, when he suddenly said: "I now doubt the advisability of turning the classroom into an encounter group." This I could neither understand nor believe. I was paralyzed with wonder by this dizzyingly retrogressive conclusion.

My horror was altogether premature and unnecessary, however. Two sentences later, Schutz redeemed himself entirely by saying: "I think the intensive group experience is probably best handled for school youth in a camp or similar setting, away from the school." All was well. The May 7 cadre schools are not found in Peking. They are found in some wasteland far from the corrupting influence of the city, and this is as it should be.

A particularly interesting example of what can happen when the proponents of the H.P.M. become influential in an organization was the Annual Staff Conference of the Addiction Research Foundation of Ontario on February 28, 1972. This event took place at a Y.M.C.A. retreat in an idyllic setting on the shore of Lake Couchiching, many miles from the home bases of any of the participants.

The conference was introduced under the title, "Perspectives '72", but it was generally understood to bear a direct historical relationship to previous staff conferences of the foundation.

About a hundred people came accordingly from all parts of the province to attend the Annual Staff Conference. The theme of this meeting, they had been told, was to be "change". The organizers had been persuaded that this was a topic highly relevant to the work of the A.R.F. Before anyone arrived they had received excerpts from the work of several authors, all of whom had won fortune in recent years from their espousal of either magic humanism or what has been called "futures research". Thus the participants got reprints from Gardner (*Self-Renewal: the Individual and the Innovative Society*), Hunter (*The Enemies of Anarchy*) and Toffler (*Future Shock*). Moreover the conference was to offer a number of statements by various people on the nature and significance of change and on measures that might be used by people in their attempts to adapt to such potentially distressing circumstances. The participants were vulnerable, therefore, in the sense that they were not given any information regarding the actual intentions of the organizers. The organizers, on the other hand, were very secretive because their real intent was to conduct a surprise experiment. For this they were determined to use the staff members who had come voluntarily and in good faith to the retreat.

I will briefly describe this event, but it is my main purpose at this point to emphasize that what happened was a perfectly natural extension of the process begun several years earlier in the A.R.F. and which had been dignified all that time under the rubric of Organizational Development. This programme had been persistently described as being very conservative and benign. Indeed it had been specifically denied that what happened at the Quetico Centre, the retreat ordinarily used by the foundation, could in any sense be described as sensitivity training. Nevertheless the incident at Lake Couchiching might have been predicted from the beginning. The belief that, regardless of its value, innovation is essential in any organization frequently leads to absurdity and excess.

On the first morning of the conference it was announced that breakfast was to be in a new location: participants gathered for that purpose. Breakfast did not appear, however. Instead, staff members were invited to enter an adjoining room where they were seated as though to hear a prepared speech. This speech was delivered by a psychologist who was particularly interested in the encounter movement. A number of participants subsequently described his speech as being intentionally disjointed and tiresome: of particular interest was the fact that during its delivery the temperature of the room was raised to about ninety degrees. Following his discourse the speaker remained at the microphone and from this position instructed the participants to move their chairs to the sides of the room. One chair, he said, would remain in the centre.

The participants were instructed to mill about this chair; the lights became very dim; loud music and traffic noises were heard. The leader continued to speak, but now, as a number of participants observed, his voice was emanating from a tape recorder on the other side of the room.

The reader will have already recognized that the change-agent was conducting a variety of the manipulative technique known as the microlab, developed by Schutz at Esalen. Some participants moved to the side of the room and a few left altogether, in spite of exhortations by assistants at the doors to stay and co-operate. The great majority, however, were obedient to the commands of the leader. They milled about the centre of the room, following his orders unquestioningly. In so doing they confirmed the hypothesis that a designated authority can, should he so desire, control the behaviour of his subjects, even to the point of causing them to act in an absurd and childlike manner.

Finally the tape recorder was switched off and the participants were instructed to sit on the floor a few feet away from each other. The lights went up and soft music was heard. In this crude and unsophisticated display, we may observe the application of a basic technique of behaviour control. Sensory over-stimulation was alternated with a period of relative sensory deprivation in a setting in which there was a strong leader and much encouragement to be conformist and compliant.

The leader now assured the participants that he had intentionally humiliated them. He had denied them food, made them listen to a confusing address in an over-heated room, caused them to mill about while cacophony proceeded from a tape recorder in a corner of the darkness. Now he instructed them to go to their small, pre-arranged groups to discuss, in purely affective terms, *how they felt* about the events of the morning.

The members of the planning committee arranging this experiment had presumably achieved their purpose. They had demonstrated that men and women could be abused by duly constituted authority. And they had demonstrated that this could easily be done even among educated, intelligent and free people who were members of both a helping agency and a liberal-democratic society. They had done this, so they said, because they wanted to offer a graphic illustration of the conference theme. We must not fail to recognize, however, that the techniques used by these people to achieve their purpose were directly taken from the encounter movement (and from the long history of evangelism and political demagoguery). Though they may have been naive, these men were not blameless. They presumed to play with the sensibilities of people who, in the circumstances, were not quite classifiable as volunteers. However briefly, they created a mass out of these individual people. Then they guided this mass according to the dictates of their own pleasure. The humanity of the participants was reduced; their dignity was affected.

In the jargon of orgment, a person is expected to "deselect" himself when, in the course of his training, he comes to recognize that his goals and objectives are discordant with those of the organization. That is to say he is expected to gracefully resign. Instead of doing the proper thing, I wrote a critical paper because I genuinely felt that this exercise was a grave misapplication of authority. I distributed copies of it to certain key people within the foundation. The following day I was dismissed for what were described as purely budgetary reasons.

Still another interesting observation can be made on the basis of this incident. If everything contained in my written paper had been expressed orally in the setting of one of the confrontation groups following the morning's session, it is unlikely that any action would have been taken. This is another and most illuminating illustration of the fear magic humanists have for the written as opposed to the spoken word. The latter is ephemeral, however charged it may be with affect; the written word is conserved, and its influence persists long after the moment of its selection.

Now it is quite true that some of the participants reported later that it was all just a game and that as such it was rather fun. Others said it was a bit infantile and silly but a matter of no consequence, it was simply better to comply for the short duration of the experiment. A few were profoundly distressed by the experience, however. Some people profoundly appreciate privacy, living space, and individuality. They abhor pressing and noisy crowds, but they are not sick on this account. Some have studied the techniques of sensitivity training and concluded that these do not please them personally. On being surprised by their involuntary inclusion in a variant of the encounter game these people might become quite resentful.

Indeed in the days that followed a great deal of anger was directed at the organizers of this affair.

One other matter is of some interest. A small but significant incident took place in one of the group sessions that immediately followed the Schutzian demonstration. One of the people who had been intensely offended by the behaviour of the leader and his assistants expressed his resentment and concern in the course of this group session. He reported: "I must note that my behaviour was on one occasion labelled as 'schizoid' by a senior staff psychiatrist. He hastened to add that this could be construed as a healthy reaction and should not be confused with 'pre-schizophrenic'. Nonetheless, it did seem to make it easier for others in the group to add 'paranoid' to the description of my behaviour."

This psychiatrist participated in the small group as an ordinary staff member indistinguishable from everybody else. Yet for all that, he was an eminent man with many degrees and appointments. When such a person speaks he does so from the position of the learned specialist. When he offers a diagnosis in a public gathering his words are undeniably freighted with a particular significance according to the rank he has achieved in the course of long study. Now the participant who had expressed his resentment concerning the manipulative techniques of the leader had done so because he did not find the spectacle arranged by the foundation expressive of the dignity of man. His negative reaction was diagnosed by a learned doctor as an indication of a schizoid personality. Those who, with this doctor, had milled mindlessly about the chair to the sound of the traffic noises and the recorded voice of the leader were presumably behaving in a manner indicative of enlightenment, and great security against any loss of identity and human worth.

My final point is that this exchange may be seen as a small expression of the insensitivity of those members of the H.P.M. who constantly emphasize the crucial necessity of encouraging sensitivity. These people, insisting that it is their desire to enhance creativity and improve interpersonal relationships, are fundamentally authoritarian although, it is true, this urge is masked by a system of words and ideas that imply precisely the opposite.

It is the objective of the movement to create the authentic person; and the nature of this state is so self-evident and so virtuous that any opposition to this view is intolerable. In fact such non-conformity is identified as maladaptive. In the Human Potential Movement the immersion of the self in the group is essential; he who resists this process is regarded as divisive and anti-social. He may then be identified as "schizoid", because this is one of the meanings of that useless but emotionally charged word. If he protests and expresses hostility towards the trainers who, with the full support of the organization, are promoting group regression, he may then be identified as "paranoid". He is projecting his own interior anger.

Such diagnoses are most commonly made by the trainers who, as I have pointed out on many occasions, are often exceedingly unqualified as clinicians. It is especially significant, then, when a learned psychiatrist publicly utters the same diagnosis: a man who resists his own humiliation is "schizoid". What is particularly distressing about all such exercises is that they are carried out in the name of education. It is the "new education", to be sure, and the aim is to prepare people for the new schools and the new social agencies. And this requires the assistance of yet another group of consultants who are pleased to call themselves futurists.

A futurist is a very giddy man who is shocked into mindless ecstasy each time he comes upon yet another horror waiting to disrupt the lives of everyone. He shrieks that this new invention will create such a state of instability that only he who can adapt to a condition of total transience will have any chance of survival. The futurist knows nothing of the upsets and catastrophes that have afflicted mankind for as long as we have been living on the planet. He assures us that we are the first people in all time to be threatened by total disaster.

In 1348, there were about sixty thousand people living within the walls of London. Nearly all were very poor, and the poor had no beds. It was usual for a dozen people, some chickens, pigs, and dogs, to sleep on the dirt floor of a single room.

The lanes were wide enough to allow two donkeys to pass, and the houses grew wider with each storey. Very little light penetrated to the mud of the lanes and the open sewers running down their centres. Slop, excrement and garbage were thrown continuously from the tenements into the streets, and the rain was counted on to wash all this detritus into London's river.

The people had no privacy, hardly anything to call their own, and their very short lives were afflicted with dysentry and hunger. The black rat flourished in the houses built of clay and wood, and in the dirt and offal that was everywhere. The black rat carried the bubonic plague, and by 1349 about thirty thousand people had died in London.

William of Dene wrote in that year that "a plague of a kind which had never been met with before ravaged our land of England. . . . To our great grief the plague carried off so vast a multitude of people that nobody could be found who would bear the corpses to the grave. Men and women carried their own children on their shoulders to the church and threw them into a common pit. From these pits such an appalling stench was given off that scarcely anyone dared even to walk beside the cemeteries.

"During the whole of that winter the bishop . . . remained (at his country manor) bewailing the terrible changes which had overcome the world."

The whole world was, for the bishop, a small part of the southeast of England. It is the terror that matters and not the number of people or the vastness of the area affected. The insecurity with which the people of Europe were afflicted for the thirty years during which plague kept returning was greater by far than anything that the totality of our people today are called upon to face. The shrill voices of our futurists, telling us that the computers are coming and that we must urgenty adapt to a life of continuous change, sound very silly when we realize that Londoners have endured far greater threats from plagues and fires and bombs, and have always managed somehow to survive. What could be a more absolute source of horror than the awful presence of the black death in your hovel in London, in 1348?

There is an immense difference between the security of our lives and that of medieval man. We are aware of the possibility of sickness and death but there is usually a certain remoteness about these things. We do not really believe that we will become sick and die today or even next year. In the 14th Century every man knew that he, his wife and his children, might suffer some trivial injury and be crippled or killed by infection at any moment. To us the futurists offer the dread thought that at some remote time we may be spindled by a computer. Very few of us, I must suggest, live in constant anguish on the basis of this or most of the other predictions of the futurists. Nor was it only medieval man who was afflicted with perpetual fear of imminent catastrophe. Until only a few decades ago superstition and ineffectual medicine crowded the lives of everyone. If we live in an age of anxiety today, then all previous ages must have been times of utter dread.

Yet we are constantly assured that momentous innovations in technology have unnerved the people. Satellites now whirl about the earth and this, it is said, has created a global village. By cloning, a whole series of identical animals can be created from the cells of the intestinal tract of a single donor. But what do the people actually worry about? Do they worry about the threat of atomic annihilation?

They do not. The people worry about their personal health, their relationships with their spouses, children and colleagues, and their persistent debts. They worry about their own safety and that of their closest relatives. The sort of change that absolutely swamps them has nothing to do with any of the things futurists talk about. It is the death of their wives, the threat of separation or divorce, or the ill health of someone very close to them that causes them depression and anxiety. They are not overwhelmed when they learn that a thousand frogs can be made from a single frog, and that therefore a thousand Hitlers could be made from a single Hitler. They are overwhelmed when they are fired, or find themselves in trouble with the law, or discover that a girl friend is unaccountably pregnant. These are the things that cause discomfort in the greatest number of the people as they live through the days of their lives. And it follows from this that these people desire as much social stability and public safety as it is possible to arrange.

Such people have developed permanent attachments to people and places, and the main outlines of their careers are relatively clear to them. They can even predict the future with some degree of accuracy. In fact they have, through their considerable efforts, imposed a certain familiarity on their environment, and they are progressively less receptive to influences that would surprise them and force them into circumstances that are strange, and therefore forbidding. Culture, for them, has continuity in all of its diverse aspects.

This statement, at any rate, is not untrue if it refers to the majority of people. It is certainly untrue if it refers to the intellectual and artistic elite. In the course of the last few decades these people have become progressively more savage in their assault on the great institutions of the society.

In Greenwich Village, in Chelsea and on the Left Bank a marked response to the allegedly dehumanizing threat of technology was made. In these places the artistic avant garde began to emphasize spontaneity and immediacy. What was frail and accidental in man was admired. The irrational was particularly honoured. Indeed any tendency that seemed antithetical to the organizing, planning and circumscribing influence of technology was emphasized. A certain life style began to emerge in the Bohemian quarters of a few large cities. In all the arts the nonsensical became important. Plays were written that rejected all of the Aristotelian principles of plot, characterization, conflict, and dénouement. Novels became similarly formless. Realism was specifically held to be irrelevant to art. The traditional or linear style in which a sequence of logically related ideas or images would be presented by the artist was replaced by the mosaic style in which the effect was always one of fragmentation and intentional unrelatedness. The artist abandoned his intellect and came to rely on intuitive bursts of insight and sudden accidents of the pen or the brush. The content of art also began to change. As in every romantic revival there was a new emphasis on the erotic, the deviant, the absurd, and finally on the menacing. The artists regarded themselves as living works of art and therefore their lives were similarly unrestrained and ideally accidental.

During this same period the social and political theorists were equally concerned to vilify the institutions of the society. The family unit was particularly condemned, and the authority that was previously vested in parents was greatly reduced. In the course of time more and more responsibility was assigned to the schools to establish guidelines for living in the world: but teachers were afflicted with the same fear that had paralyzed the parents. The child must not be restrained. He must be free to express his personality in any way that seemed most natural for him to do. He must be offered a thousand choices and from these, through the exercise of his adolescent judgment, he must select those that would lead to the fullest expression of his native ability. The crucial importance of experience began to be emphasized and from this an essentially hedonistic philosophy gained wide support. Such antique notions as goal-directed activity and the postponement of gratification were scorned both in the schools and in many homes. No one, it was held, should be paternalistic. It was a reprehensible expression of the authoritarian impulse.

In physiology there is a basic process known as homeostasis. This means that if some functional imbalance develops, a sequence of responses occurs to counteract this tendency. If blood pressure falls, the heart automatically beats more strongly, and the small vessels of the periphery constrict. The result of this negative response to the original stimulus is an improvement in blood pressure. If, on the other hand, the heart should beat less strongly in response to low blood pressure, its reaction would reinforce the original tendency: this would be incompatible with life.

Analagously, if certain technological developments bring about alienation and threaten individuality the most injurious of all possible responses would be to produce a literature that promotes alienation and discontent and offers as The Answer the illusion of self-realization in the group. That would be a perfect expression of positive reinforcement which, as I have suggested, is certain to cause worsening of the very condition it was supposed to treat. The short-sightedness is not, as the potentialists would have us believe, all on the side of the old culture. The insinuation of the H.P.M. into every aspect of our society is demonstrably not benign, and yet its proponents continue to claim that its techniques must be used if what they have diagnosed as our sick society is to be saved. Prescribing sugar for a diabetic would be no more helpful than prescribing an encounter for a person whose defences are poorly designed to meet the ordinary challenges of life. More stress, and the systematic tearing down of his defences, are clearly not what such a person needs.

By the same token it is quite depressing to hear learned futurists proclaiming to millions of people on television that the educational system is valueless, and deploring the fact that the children feel alienated from the educational system. These great men, I must point out, are specialists in the issuance of self-fulfilling prophecies. It is also of some interest that the urge to make ill-judged and ignorant statements of this sort is strongly reinforced by the processes of attitudinal reorientation practised within even the least excessive manifestations of the human potential movement.

Of all arguments against the unrestrained expansion of the H.P.M. the most cogent, in my view, is that its techniques do indeed cause attitudinal change; and that this change appears always to be in the direction of disinhibition, rejection of the values of the inclusive society, and the belief that the real human being, the really creative human being, is the one who dislikes competence, integrity and self-control, and who admires the spontaneous expression of feeling regardless of the circumstances. An ideology that especially values childlike patterns of behaviour, and that specifically rejects the distinctions between the intelligent and the dull, the learned and the ignorant, the refined and the vulgar, is an ideology that has no interest in excellence. It is interested in mediocrity.

The Human Potential Movement offers such an ideology, and out of this has designed its own utopia. In fact the movement shows many characteristics of the millennial cult. Its adherents, converts to this futurist vision, are very busy proselytizing and urging the sudden abandonment of what they call the old culture.

The range of this attack is altogether remarkable. It is certainly no longer the case that sensitivity training is available only in a few hundred specialized growth centres and social agencies. A number of books have been written by enthusiastic encounterists and in these may be found detailed descriptions of the many games that are said to bring about sensory awareness. Moreover it is now possible to buy encounter tapes that are designed to be used by leaderless groups. One such tape begins with what are called "impressions". A disembodied voice tells the group to form a circle and have each member approach every other member to tell him precisely what he thinks of him. Another tape describes the break-in, break-out game and a whole series of similar activities.

A third tape is called "trust", and describes a game in which the person in the centre of the circle closes his eyes and is passed around on the hands of his fellows. Since they do not tend to drop him he learns about trust. I am reminded of an ancient joke in which a father tells his son to stand on a table and jump. The son does so, and the father catches him. With a few repetitions of this exercise the son is conditioned to accept that jumping is a perfectly safe thing to do. Finally, however, when the son jumps, the father steps back. The son hits the floor with a great thump. Shattered in body and mind, the boy looks up poignantly at his evil parent, only to hear: "That'll learn ya not to trust nobody, not even yer own father!"

I am not unaware that basic trust is an essential ingredient in any close relationship, but it is a certainty that in the great wide world the naive and gullible person will soon be victimized by those who are shrewd, and perhaps a bit unscrupulous. For example, an innocent person might be preyed upon by an encounterist offering him creativity and wisdom through the exercise of his midbrain.

Pop psych has passed beyond the encounter-tape phase. There is a soft-cover book on the market called *Conduct your own Awareness Sessions,* and this work is widely available. There are also a number of ingenious party games that have, I understand, sold quite well. In the case of "Sensitivity" the six or seven players are each given folders outlining a fictitious case history. The player is then expected to take the part of this alcoholic mother, debtor or cuckold, and in so doing be as convincing as possible. If he fails the other players may award him the "Ghengis Khan Memorial Trophy for the invasion of privacy on all fronts, while keeping your own frontiers intact".

The invention called "Group Therapy" is described as a game "for people who want to do more than just play games". This is an item for real adults. The players are all given judge's cards marked "with it" on one side and "cop out" on the other. The first player takes the top card from a stack of "therapy cards" and reads it aloud. He then has exactly one minute to perform the instruction, which might be, "Hold each member of the group in a way which shows how you feel about him," or, "Stand up. Select someone. Go totally limp in his arms." The card that seems to me to be the most therapeutic is the one that reads: "Pick a way in which you are phoney and exaggerate it."

After each performance, the other players turn their cards to indicate "cop out" or "with it" and the player moves his token on the board according to the result of this judgment. "Was he glib? Did he try to make a joke of what he was doing?" If so, say the instructions, he was copping out, and if he keeps being "afraid to be vulnerable" like that, he will never make it to "free". All that is needed is a liberated host, a party game, and a group of willing guests.

These games represent one extreme. They are the *reductio ad absurdum* of the personal growth ideas of poor Kurt Lewin and the N.T.L. people of the late 'forties. We should now consider another extreme, the monstrous corruption of the ideas of poor Douglas McGregor who wanted only to make management more humane, and more responsive to the needs of the employees.

In a totalitarian state the manipulators of human beings have certain techniques of persuasion available to them that are not allowable in our society. They can threaten to torture a man who resists resocialization, and they can proceed to carry out this threat. They can even execute a wilful client. The knowledge that such power is available to the expediter undoubtedly has a marked effect on the motivation of the schoolmates.

On agreeing with me that the success of the Quetico Centre in bringing about organizational excellence was very limited, a strong supporter of the orgment programme said: "It is not working because it is not being pursued with sufficient vigour." He was absolutely right. If a programme is to really work it must be utterly radical, and therefore utterly ruthless. It must take all the exercises of the movement and exaggerate them as extremely as it is possible to do.

In our society such a programme has been carried out by an organization known as Leadership Dynamics Institute. The story of L.D.I. is an astonishing one. It is the creation of William Penn Patrick, a businessman who used the techniques of pyramid selling to make a cosmetics company known as Holiday Magic Inc. an immensely successful affair. Patrick initially set up a series of training sessions for Holiday Magic executives based on his book, *Happiness and Success through Principle.* These seminars were designed to cause participants to face their deficiencies and anxieties so that they might become more creative, live more constructive lives, and become more efficient salesmen for the company. In 1969, Patrick offered the course to the general public, and by the middle of 1972 about two thousand people in several countries had experienced the L.D.I. encounter. Throughout this period the course continued to evolve, and not all these people endured the ultimate version of it that is described here.

There were usually about twenty-five people at an L.D.I.

seminar, all of whom had paid $1,000 in advance to attend the four-day marathon session. They were paired and told that if one member of a pair left the motel and did not return, the remaining member would be ejected and lose his money. Since it was generally understood that advancement in the company was dependent on attendance, this factor, as well as the possibility of a considerable financial loss, tended to motivate people to remain to the end. They also stayed, however, because they genuinely felt that the experience was the most important thing that had ever happened to them. The instructors at L.D.I. specialized in bringing about the peak experience.

Before the marathon began the members of the class were required to sign a general release which, in effect, gave the instructors the right to do just about anything they wished to do. In the course of the next four days very little time was allowed for sleeping, and food was given sparingly.

The seminar was held in the wing of a motel. In a lounge area adjoining the sleeping quarters the chairs were arranged to create a central open space. This area was described as The Pit and there one student after another was stripped naked and subjected to an interrogation that might go on for several hours. The student was tormented by the instructor but also, most significantly, by the other students, who were advised to assist in the badgering. Various bits of information would be introduced by the instructor concerning, for example, the student's affair with a Holiday Magic girl in his home town which, as far as he knew, had been entirely secret. The student would be asked about this matter repeatedly until he confessed to the truth of it. The decision might then be made to punish him not only for the crime of adultery but also for the far graver crime of not being open and honest. He would accordingly be punched by the instructor with great severity, and then paddled mercilessly by the group until he wept in pain.

In a corner of the room there was a coffin, used from time to time when it was decided that a man needed to be shown that he was so lacking in spontaneity he might as well be dead. He might be put inside with the lid closed on him for many hours. If on the other hand a student was judged to be alive but lacking in manliness he might have a wire turned tightly around his testicles to dramatize his preoccupation with psychic castration.

In another part of the room there was a cage which was used to indicate that a student lived his life as though he were a helpless and dependent prisoner. Such a student might spend a half day or so in this small wire enclosure. There was also a hangman's noose and from time to time a student might be made to stand with his head in it. There was a wooden cross large enough to accommodate a man who felt that in his regular life he ordinarily suffered such cruel and unusual punishment. Strung up on this cross for a couple of hours, he might experience the reality of crucifixion.

In the course of the seminar each student was to be tormented, beaten and humiliated until he achieved a state of total honesty. When, at last, that point had been reached, the instructor would shout: "He's a man at last!" The assembly would hug him and he was led ceremonially past the silver chalice, the symbol of truth and honesty.

An extraordinarily graphic account of one of these L.D.I. seminars was written by Gene Church, who actually participated in such a marathon in Palo Alto, California. His book, *The Pit,* is a remarkable document. Church and his co-writer Conrad Carnes, began by describing the opening remarks of the chief instructor. The chalice was going to be found by every man present, but it would not be easy to reach. L.D.I. was going to do whatever was necessary in order to bring each student to the moment of truth. The instructor walked to the man nearest to him and asked the class what he would do if it was necessary to pat this man on the back in order to make him find honesty within himself. The class said that the instructor would pat him on the back. This was done. The instructor approached the next man and asked what he would do if it was necessary to kiss this man on the head in order to make him honest. Again the class responded to the effect that the instructor would kiss him on the head. This too was done.

The instructor then moved to a third man and said: "If it's necessary, gentlemen, for us to beat the shit out of someone until he can't think straight enough to lie, what do you think we're going to do?" Church reported here that the class was stunned, but finally a few members agreed that that was exactly what the instructor would do. According to Church, the instructor "then positioned himself directly in front of Schwartz, drew back and with a full swing hit Schwartz squarely in the face".

The rest of the seminar was an astonishing procession of violence and humiliation. Men were beaten, forced to carry out degrading sexual acts, caged, and throttled to the point of unconsciousness. *Newsweek* magazine quoted Patrick as saying: "We created different situations to make different points to the class. Concrete symbols drive the points home. Unless it is powerfully presented it doesn't get driven home." L.D.I. illustrates in great detail the ultimate perversion of the principles of organization development.

10

In Defence of the Individual

Very little can be done to protect people against their involvement in the parlour-game variety of sensitivity training. In fact all that can be done is to advise people that if they play these games they are exposing themselves to the possibility of psychic distress. These games are, of course, manifestations of the faddist aspect of the movement, and their popularity may not long continue.

Similarly, anyone can read the literature of the H.P.M. and be immensely impressed by it if his inclinations run along those lines. It is exceedingly clear, however, that the movement has been very appealing and even receptive to charlatans, and it may be that something can be done to inhibit the work of these people. In the 19th Century the bodies of our people were preyed upon indiscriminately by the travelling medicine men. These quacks were controlled finally by the passing of patent medicine laws. Today the minds of the people are being treated by a new breed of root doctor in a manner that closely resembles the style of the 19th-century entrepreneurs. Fraud, regrettably, is difficult to prove when all the leader claims to offer is warmth, understanding and a bit of human interaction.

It is the human growth centres, the personnel departments, and the schools that may be subjected to certain restraints.

1. *Screening*

Screening, for example, is almost never carried out, yet it is known that a great many people are not liable to benefit from sensitivity training and may even be hurt by it. Before a person is introduced to a potentially harmful physical treatment today it is generally accepted that he will first be examined by someone competent to determine his capacity to withstand this treatment. Our minds are no less sensitive than our bodies, and we do have in our society a great many specialists in both normal and abnormal psychology who might well be expected to successfully identify people particularly liable to become casualties.

2. *The Principle of Informed Consent*

At the very least the person should be told precisely what it is that he is getting into. Yet this very requirement is avoided by many group leaders on the grounds that the sudden introduction of a particular game might be specifically helpful, in their opinion, at a particular point in time. The value of this technique would depend, they insist, on its being introduced as a surprise. Its existence cannot be revealed in advance of the session. This is entirely unacceptable. Each participant must be told who the trainers will be, what techniques will be used, and what the purpose of the programme is felt to be. The participants must also be informed that confidentiality cannot be guaranteed in sessions of this type.

It is not only the techniques that might be used, however, that must interest us. The subject should also be apprised of the social attitude of his trainer. This is not irrelevant because, as I have indicated, the trainer's position may be decidedly radical. This is something that it would be useful for the trainee to know. In organization development, for example, it is never revealed in advance of the management seminar that the trainers believe the economic, liberal democratic, judicial, and educational systems of the larger society are archaic and injurious. Yet these trainers commonly hold that this is so. No less than any other agent of the movement, O.D. is concerned to dig up the very roots of society.

All these growth centres seem devoted to this sacred cause and their endeavours will not soon become less vigorous. The principle of informed consent would require that every prospective trainee be told in as much detail as possible what philosophic and political systems are subscribed to by the centre. In this society we watch our elected representatives very closely and expect from them the fullest disclosure of their views on political questions. We should be especially watchful, therefore, of those trainers who have appointed themselves to oppose the basic institutions of our society. It would certainly not be unreasonable for us to expect that they, too, should disclose their political views and their intentions. Openness, they must be reminded, does in fact have a very basic application in some areas of the free society.

3. *Freedom of Choice*

This, too, will be difficult for the movement, because freedom of choice is antithetical to their basic position. One cannot promote infantile behaviour and claim at the same time that he is honouring the integrity of the individual. In the group the deviant member is the person who does not conform to the desires of the group. Deviation is intolerable and group pressure is specifically brought to bear on that person to assist him to achieve joy and total conformity. Finally, if the marathon session lasts long enough, his fatigue will be such that he will break, and weep, and beg for forgiveness and support. There is no person in the world who could not be brought to a state of abject surrender.

The individual should be absolutely free to leave the group at any time he so desires. This becomes a particularly difficult problem in the case of organization development because there the client is an employee, and his employer is deeply committed to an expensive programme that requires total acceptance. The employee who does not conform to the increasingly more persuasive techniques used by the organization will not be caused to feel more secure in his job. He may imagine that those people who are more agreeable will be favoured in the future. This is an intolerable state of affairs. Participation must at all times be strictly voluntary.

It is apparent that many of the techniques used in the movement are experimental. Indeed it is considered a particular achievement to have invented a new technique or at least a new variety of an existing one. The techniques are then used immediately on human subjects, and this constitutes a very serious action. It is now widely accepted in medicine that no person should be subjected to an experimental procedure unless three basic criteria are satisfied. The subject must give his consent after being told everything that is known about the technique under examination. His participation as an experimental subject must be absolutely voluntary. And finally, there must be some underlying theory that supports the experiment and justifies its being carried out in the first place. In the case of, for example, sensitivity training sessions in Grade 6 classrooms in which the teacher is inspired to be furiously innovative, all three criteria may be violated. It is remarkable, really, that those who claim to particularly value human feelings should be so callous in their treatment of the mind.

It is precisely because many of these techniques are potent that they must not be used unless all of these conditions are satisfied. There are by now, as we have seen, hundreds of these games. Each new leader seems to be driven to devise a new one to add to the many he learned in the course of his own training. And all these techniques are designed to promote childlike and dependent behaviour. They facilitate regression in adults. They are intensely opposed to the conscious operation of the intellect.

In fact the similarity between hypnosis and the techniques of group interaction is very striking. It has sometimes occurred to me that if the employees in an office were informed that they must undergo a series of hypnotic trances in the interests of organizational excellence they might well resist. In fact their sense of outrage would be very clearly expressed. They would imagine that this constituted a deliberate attempt on the part of their employer to use a behaviour-control technique to reduce their independence and make them more compliant. They would also be afraid that the deeply personal information that might be gained in the course of the experience might be entered in their records by the employer. This information might then be used to determine their further advance, or lack of it, in the organization. Many people would feel it was not the employer's right to have such an intimate familiarity with the personal lives of his employees.

Hypnosis depends for its effectiveness on its tendency to promote suggestibility. Every one of the techniques of sensitivity training also depends on the promotion of heightened suggestibility. These are behaviour-control techniques just as surely as is hypnosis. If the employees were asked to submit voluntarily to sodium pentothal abreaction techniques they would again resist. They do not tend to resist O.D. because they are not told anything about the nature of the techniques that will be used, and of their ultimate similarity to so many other techniques that are well known to modify behaviour and to elicit personal information.

It is fascinating to me to note that whenever such remarks as I have just made are heard by a potentialist he quickly counters with the presumably devastating word "paranoid". Paranoid indeed. This is too facile a response. There is absolutely no doubt that a great many of the workers in a corporation or in a branch of government are seriously concerned about such matters as the loss of privacy, a state gained only recently in our society, and much valued. If the proponents of orgment would cease their easy reiteration of their favourite word for just a moment they might come to realize that delusional thinking is not so common in the general population. There are, in fact, very real problems concerning the use of sensitivity training in work places, and particularly in schools, and not every critic is a madman. Quite a number of people regard themselves as individuals and are determined to defend themselves against any influence that threatens to diminish the quality of that condition. If orgment is benign and even useful then let there be some convincing evidence that these things are true. If it is neither benign nor useful then let it be engaged in only by those who are diverted by novel experiences and who care not at all about the possibility of injury.

4. *Precautions*

The leader, and the centre, must always be able to provide services for the treatment of physical and psychiatric injuries. This requirement is frequently not satisfied. On the role of the leader, Parloff is especially concise: "The skilled therapist is careful to permit an optimal level of regression, namely, a level which does not overwhelm the patient's capacity to utilize primary process materials constructively. The skills required in the stimulation of regression and, more importantly, in the promotion of the effective use of such material . . . cannot be assumed to be present in the casually-trained or untrained encounter group leader." He concludes by noting that the leader must also be able to handle the crises that arise from time to time. He must also be willing to exclude from the group any person whose presence is unduly threatening to the others.

The professional competence of the leader is very much at issue here. T-groups and encounters are most frequently run by people who are under no obligation whatsoever to conform to the basic ethical requirements of some professional organization. Indeed in the movement there is generally much contempt for such learned societies on the grounds that their tendency is to be elitist and intellectual.

5. *Follow-Up*

There are many problems associated with the termination of the group and the re-entry of the person into society. These might be reduced if a plan for systematic follow-up were incorporated into the design of the programme. The value of this suggestion in terms of research must also be apparent.

It is frequently suggested that one of the essential functions of the group movement is to counteract the loneliness that is said to be characteristic of our society. Yet the group does not seem to achieve this effect. The people come together and become intensely involved with one another for a few hours or weeks: then they depart and seldom meet again.

It is a matter of the greatest importance that restraints be established on the use of these several techniques. In fact there are a great many intelligent and responsible people working in this field today and it would be to their advantage if the charlatans found their activity curtailed. It has not been conclusively proven by any means, but it would seem that there is a place for some of the methods of therapy developed within the H.P.M. They should be examined very carefully, tested, and put to proper use.

Those elements of the movement that are obviously disruptive to the society, and that threaten the security of the majority of the people, should no longer be encouraged. As always, such cells will be tolerated by the general society, and this is as it should be in a pluralistic culture, but they should not be accorded the salvationist status they have enjoyed for rather too long. Those things that are absurd should be identified as such and treated as befits such trivial and amusing aberrations. The Schutzian speculum and the cant of the wordless specialist in communication arts are in this category.

The point is that it should no longer be necessary for anyone to be in awe of these marvellous innovators. It is necessary on the other hand for individual people to notice that some things are ludicrous or ignorant or humiliating and for them to say, very loudly, that this is so. No one today should have to uncritically accept as a leader and seer a man to whom he has not been introduced and whose ideas are seriously contrary to his own. In particular he should not have to agree that he be subjected to group pressure that might cause him to give up certain freedoms which, in other circumstances, he would fight to preserve.

As has been said, the leaders appear to be protected against the charge of malpractice because they contend that they are not engaged in therapy. We should expect, however, that people who have been physically or mentally injured through their participation in sensitivity training will elect to charge these injuries to the leader and to the organization for which he works.

According to Maliver the first such legal action against the movement occurred in late 1970. This was the case of a woman who worked for the U.S. Department of Health, Education and Welfare. The department had recommended that she attend an encounter session: she did so, and was asked to demonstrate physical aggression with another member. She was thrown to the floor and injured. She filed a suit for $500,000 against the sponsor of the programme. Since that time a number of actions have been brought against various leaders and organizations for allowing physical injuries, and I do not doubt that it will be this development that will particularly restrain the more enthusiastic purveyors of aggressive joy. The Leadership Dynamics Institute has had several lawsuits to contend with, some of which have already been settled out of court. It seems likely that such difficulties will serve to control the excesses of physical violence that seem to be characteristic of this variety of orgment. No school board or company that has begun to implement an organizational development programme should consider itself unaccountable for what happens to its employees at the retreat.

Such an organization might be found responsible for the disruption of the life of one of its employees who held that his resignation, or lack of advancement, was directly referable to his participation in sensitivity training. Such an organization might also be charged with misusing highly personal information gained in the course of its employees' training. The organization might also be challenged with respect to the qualifications of the people it had allowed to conduct its awareness sessions.

In the case of orgment it would seem to be altogether consonant with the common practice of the general society to consult the will of the entire staff before any such programme is instituted. However, this vote should not be taken until there has been a full disclosure of the reasons why it is felt that O.D. is indicated, the nature of the programme, the techniques that will be used, and the identity of the proposed consultants and trainers. Following this presentation an opportunity for open debate should be provided. Only then should the vote be taken by secret ballot. It must be understood, however, that even after the programme has been approved by the entire staff, no person should be penalized for his failure to participate in it. The voluntary nature of the programme must be guaranteed in the official policy of the institution.

Moreover this vote should be repeated annually with the understanding that the staff, duly gathered together for this purpose, may order the discontinuation of the programme.

*　　*　　*　　*

The ancient problems of man will not be solved by a new emphasis on one of his most ancient solutions. Yet the intense revival of interest in this solution has always been an indication of bewilderment. In our case the power of the technocracy, the omnipotence of the machines, and the menacing evidences of the creation of an electronic utopia are some of the sources of this confusion; and the resurgence of interest in the life of the whole-earth man is clearly one possible reaction to these things. There is obviously much that is admirable and necessary about this resistance. We must, however, retain our awareness that utopian movements contain within them a pervasive urge towards authoritarianism. The cure, in other words, could be as awful as the disease. We face two major threats. The technological tyrant stands on one side and the magic humanists with their vision of simple collectivism stand on the other. Neither model of utopia as proposed by these combatants is encouraging to regard. Reason, as a god enthroned, can be as ruthless as emotion deified. In both cases it is the individuality and sanity of man that is most seriously threatened.

In *The Undiscovered Self* Carl Jung wrote: "Resistance to the organized mass can be effected only by the man who is as well organized in his individuality as the mass itself." This could be a guide to all those who are frightened by the machine and find themselves attracted by the sirens of the Earth Culture. They might be warned that the tribe is as oppressive a master as the machine.

BIBLIOGRAPHY

Allport, Gordon W., *The Nature of Prejudice*. Garden City, N.Y., Anchor Books, 1958.

Argyris, Chris, *Interpersonal Competence and Organizational Effectiveness*. Homewood, Ill., Richard D. Irwin, 1962.

Aron, Raymond, *The Opium of the Intellectuals*. New York, W. W. Norton, 1962.

Asch, S. E., "Effects of Group Pressure upon the Modification and Distortion of Judgments," in *Readings in Social Psychology*, edited by Guy E. Swanson and others. New York, Holt, Rinehart and Winston, 1952, pp. 2-10.

Blake, Robert R., Mouton, Jane S., *The Managerial Grid*. Houston, Tex., Gulf Publishing, 1964.

Blake, Robert R., Mouton, Jane S., *Corporate Excellence Diagnosis*. Austin, Tex., Scientific Methods, 1968.

Bradford, Leland P., Gibb, J., and Benne, K., eds., *T-Group Theory and Laboratory Method: Innovation in Re-education*. New York, John Wiley and Sons, 1964.

Brown, James A. C., *Techniques of Persuasion*. Baltimore, Md., Penguin Books, 1963.

Brown, Norman O., *Love's Body*. New York, Vintage Books, 1966.

Bucke, Richard M., *Cosmic Consciousness*. New York, E. P. Dutton, 1969.

Burton, Arthur, ed., *Encounter: The Theory and Practice of Encounter Groups*. San Francisco, Jossey-Bass, 1969.

Church, Gene, Carnes, Conrad D., eds., *The Pit*. New York, Outerbridge and Lazard, 1972.

Cohn, Norman, *The Pursuit of the Millennium*. Boulder, Colo., Paladin Press, 1970.

Elon, Amos, *The Israelis*. New York, Bantam Books, 1972.

Fried, Morton H., *The Evolution of Political Society*. New York, Random House, 1967.

Galbraith, J. K., *The New Industrial State*. Boston, Houghton Mifflin, 1967.

Godwin, George, *The Great Revivalists*. London, Franklin Watts, 1951.

Goodman, Paul, *New Reformation: Notes of a Neolithic Conservative*. New York, Vintage Books, 1971.

Gurdjieff, George I., *Meetings with Remarkable Men*. Boston, Routledge and Kegan Paul, 1963.

Gustaitis, Rasa, *Turning On*. New York, Macmillan, 1969.

Hovland, Carl I., Janis, I., and Kelley, H., *Communication and Persuasion: Psychological Studies of Opinion Change*. New Haven, Conn., Yale University Press, 1953.

Howard, Jane, *Please Touch: A Guided Tour of the Human Potential Movement.* New York, Dell, 1970.

Hunter, E., *Brainwashing in Red China: The Calculated Destruction of Men's Minds.* New York, Vanguard Press, 1951.

Huxley, Aldous, *The Devils of Loudun.* London, Chatto & Windus, 1970.

Huxley, Aldous, *Doors of Perception.* Baltimore, Md., Penguin Books, 1959.

James, William, *The Varieties of Religious Experience.* New York, Fontana Books, 1960.

Jonas, George, *The Happy Hungry Man.* Toronto, House of Anansi Press, 1970.

Jung, C. G., *The Undiscovered Self.* New York, The New American Library, 1959.

Katz, Daniel, Kahn, Robert L., *The Social Psychology of Organizations.* New York, John Wiley and Sons, 1966.

Kierkegaard, Soren, *Either/Or,* Vol. I., translated by Walter Lowrie. Princeton, N.J., Princeton University Press, 1971.

Levitch, H. G., *Human Behaviour and Literary Truth.* Toronto, 1972. Unpublished ms.

Lewin, Kurt, *Field Theory in Social Science.* New York, Harper and Row, 1951.

Lieberman, Morton A., Yalom, Irvin D., and Miles, Matthew B., *Encounter Groups: First Facts.* New York, Basic Books, 1973.

Malcolm, Andrew I., *The Pursuit of Intoxication.* New York, Simon and Schuster, 1972.

Malcolm, Andrew I., *The Case Against the Drugged Mind.* Toronto, Clarke, Irwin, 1973.

Maliver, Bruce, *The Encounter Game.* New York, Stein and Day, 1973.

Marcuse, Herbert, *Reason and Revolution: Hegel and the Rise of Social Theory.* Boston, Beacon Press, 1960.

McGregor, D., *The Human Side of Enterprise.* New York, McGraw-Hill, 1960.

Meerloo, Joost A. M., *The Rape of the Mind.* New York, Grossett and Dunlap, 1961.

Mills, C. Wright, *The Power Elite.* London, Oxford University Press, 1956.

Moreno, J. L., "The Cradle of Psychodrama," in *Psychodrama,* Vol. I, *Collected Papers.* Beacon, N.Y., Beacon House, 1946.

Olmsted, Michael S., *The Small Group.* New York, Random House, 1959.

Ouspensky, P. D., *A New Model of the Universe: Principles of the Psychological Method in its Application to Problems of Science, Religion and Art.* New York, Vintage Books, 1971.

Packard, Vance, *The Hidden Persuaders.* Baltimore, Md., Penguin Books, 1970.

Perls, Frederick S., *Gestalt Theory Verbatim,* edited by John O. Stevens. New York, Bantam Books, 1971.

Prince, Raymond, ed., *Trance and Possession States*. Montreal, R. M. Bucke Memorial Society, 1968.

Rogers, Carl R., *Carl Rogers on Encounter Groups*. New York, Harper and Row, 1970.

Roszak, Theodore, *The Making of a Counter Culture*. New York, Anchor Books, 1969.

Ruitenbeek, Hendrik M., *The New Group Therapies*. New York, Avon Books, 1970.

Sargant, William, *Battle for the Mind*. New York, James H. Heineman, 1957.

Schein, Edgar H., Bennis, W. G., *Personal and Organizational Change through Group Methods*. New York, John Wiley and Sons, 1965.

Schutz, William C., *Joy: Expanding Human Awareness*. New York, Grove Press, 1967.

Schutz, William C., *Here Comes Everybody*. New York, Harrow Books, 1972.

Skinner, B. F., *Beyond Freedom and Dignity*. New York, Bantam Books, 1972.

Slater, Philip E., *The Pursuit of Loneliness: America's Culture at the Breaking Point*. Boston, Beacon Press, 1970.

Solomon, Lawrence N., Berzon, Betty, eds., *The Encounter Group: Issues and Application*. Monterey, Calif., Brooks/Cole, 1970.

Standards for the Use of Laboratory Method in NTL Institute Programs. Washington, D.C., The National Training Laboratory Institute, 1967.

Sullivan, Harry S., *The Interpersonal Theory of Psychiatry*, edited by Helen S. Perry and Mary L. Gawel. New York, W. W. Norton, 1953.

Swift, Jonathan, *Gulliver's Travels*. Cleveland, Ohio, World Syndicate Publishing, 1934.

Talmon, J. L., *The Origins of Totalitarian Democracy*. London, Sphere Books, 1970.

Thoreau, Henry David, *Walden* and *On the Duty of Civil Disobedience*. New York, Mentor Press, 1957.

Toffler, Alvin, *Future Shock*. New York, Bantam Books, 1971.

Whyte, William H., *The Organization Man*. New York, Simon and Schuster, 1956.

Ziegler, Philip, *The Black Death: A Study of the Plague in 14th Century Europe*. Baltimore, Md., Penguin Books, 1970.

INDEX

Individuality, 4, 5, 12, 19, 20, 41, 102, 138
Indocrination, 47
Informed consent, 78, 174
Innovation, 6, 50, 113
Interpersonal relationships, 80, 83, 87
Interrogators, 13, 36
Involuntary participation, 48, 73, 79
Irrational belief, 5

Joachim of Fiore, 141 ff.
John Birch Society, 128
Jonas, George, 33
Judgment, distortion of, 6
Jung, Carl G., 52, 182

Kelman, Herbert, 12
Kibbutzim, 58
Kiev, Ari, 22
Kuomintang, 43

LSD, 28, 30, 32, 95
Laboratory education, 64, 78
Leadership Dynamics Institute, 170 ff.
Legal action, 180
Levitch, H. G., 33
Lewin, Kurt, 61
Liberal democracy, 38, 129
Libertarianism, 59
Lieberman, Morton, 122
Lilly, John, 27, 30, 32
Loa, 21
Loneliness, 4, 16
Ludwig, Arnold, 20

Magic humanism, 127, 128 ff., 159
Marahaj Ji, 32
Maliver, Bruce, 129, 180
Management by objectives, 71
Managerial grid training, 43, 79
Mao Tse-tung, 46, 47, 50
Marathon encounter, 45
Marcuse, Herbert, 139, 143
Marijuana, 28
Maslow, Abraham, 70, 94

Mass indoctrination, 16, 44
May 7 Cadre Schools, 48, 107, 113, 155
McGregor, Douglas, 70 ff., 92, 139
Medicine men, 30
Meditation, 26, 102
Meeson, Brian, 148
Mein Kampf, 17
Mental disequilibrium, 20
Mesmer, Antoine, 39
Messianism, 37, 121
Methodist revival, 35, 61
Milgrim, Stanley, 8
Mobs, 25
Modern industrial state, 30
Moral Re-Armament, 60
Moral worth, denial of, 42
Moreno, Jacob, 52 ff., 111
Murphy, Michael, 94
Mussolini, Benito, 144
Mysticism, 26, 29, 148

NTL (see National Training Laboratory)
Naive subjects, 6
National Socialism, 6
National Training Laboratory, 63, 69, 84, 99, 118
Natural order, 37, 38, 80
Nazi Party, 5, 16, 144
Negative reinforcement, 9
Negative sanctions, 42
Neotranscendentalism, 14
New Culture, 15, 65, 115, 131 ff., 149
Nirvana, 26
Nomadic bands, 14
Non-verbal communication, 67, 96, 104, 151
Normal waking consciousness, 20
Normlessness, 3
Nuremburg Rallies, 16

OD (see Organization Development)
Obedience, 4, 6, 8, ff., 17, 157
Obedience, measurement of, 8 ff.